THE
ETHICAL
INVESTOR

THE ETHICAL INVESTOR

HOW TO QUIT TOXIC COMPANIES AND GROW YOUR WEALTH

NICOLE HADDOW

NERO

Published by Nero,
an imprint of Schwartz Books Pty Ltd
22–24 Northumberland Street
Collingwood VIC 3066, Australia
enquiries@blackincbooks.com
www.nerobooks.com

9781760642693 (paperback)
9781743822173 (ebook)

 A catalogue record for this
book is available from the
National Library of Australia

Cover design by Kim Ferguson
Text design by Tristan Main
Typesetting by Marilyn de Castro
Seedling illustration by Visual Generation / Shutterstock

Printed in Australia by McPherson's Printing Group.

NOTE TO READERS

This publication contains the opinions and ideas of its author. It is sold with the understanding that neither the author nor the publisher is engaged in rendering legal, tax, investment, insurance, financial, accounting, or other professional advice or services. If the reader requires such advice or services, a competent professional should be consulted. Relevant laws vary from state to state. The strategies outlined in this book may not be suitable for every individual, and are not guaranteed or warranted to produce any particular results.

No warranty is made with respect to the accuracy or completeness of the information contained herein, and both the author and publisher specifically disclaim any responsibility for any liability, loss or risk, personal or otherwise, which is incurred as a consequence, directly or indirectly, of the use and application of any of the contents of this book.

For the bright-eyed little people I'm lucky
to have call me 'Aunty Nicole'

Sorry the grown-ups made a mess;
we're cleaning it up now

Contents

Introduction

I'LL BE HONEST. I hadn't planned on becoming an ethical investor, but 2020 forced it on me.

Just as the summer bushfire smoke haze had lifted, an oppressive cloud descended in the form of a pandemic. Survival mode was activated. The idea of spending my usual $22 on smashed-avocado brunches became utterly absurd to me as we were locking ourselves in our homes for an unknown period of time. Rather than hoarding rice and pasta in bulk, I hoarded money. I needed enough cash to pay my bills if my work dried up. And as a freelance writer, that was terrifyingly likely.

The combined challenges we faced in the first few months of 2020, in particular, took me to some pretty dark places. My anxiety was acute, and I know I wasn't alone in that. Watching a chunk of your continent burn and then being plunged into interminable isolation will do that. If there was any upside to being alone with my thoughts, there was time to ponder the future. A *lot*. It's disheartening to realise that even if you do survive a pandemic, many of the old issues will be there on the other side – climate change, gender inequality and the cost of living are still quite shit. But what could I do? I'd heard a bit about ethical investment, and it wasn't like I didn't have the time to do some research. I'd been entertaining the idea of moving my superannuation and getting into the share market for a while. Given the year we were having, selecting ethical options was pertinent.

In my first book, *Smashed Avocado*, with its title inspired by demographer Bernard Salt, who wrote a now famous article opining that perhaps millennials could afford property if they didn't go out for smashed-avo brunches all the time, I documented the path I took to buy my first home. In the past decade, I've gone from moving in with my parents at thirty, with $11,000 in debt, to having a property investment and no debt. I thought I was doing pretty well, but like many people, I was just a few pay cheques away from defaulting on my loan. I didn't have much money set aside for a rainy day, let alone a stormy year.

This realisation has shocked me into action. Now, I'm ready to take a good hard look at my finances, while also trying to ensure my lifestyle is contributing to the world in a positive way. As much as possible, anyway. Before I put this ethical investment plan into action, I need to seriously clean up my act and take a more holistic approach to spending, saving and investing. A regional home is on the agenda, and so is considering whether my superannuation and banking choices reflect my values. I also want to diversify my investments, adding small amounts of spare funds to shares. Not just any shares, though. Ethical shares. Shares in companies I can really get behind.

Remarkably, during 2020 work continued to flow in. I rode the 'corona-coaster' as best I could. I thought I was doing okay, until the real estate agent who managed my investment property called.

'Hi Nicole, just wanted to let you know that your tenant has given notice of intention to vacate your property.'

Bloody brilliant, I thought.

'In the middle of lockdown?' I asked, trying not to panic.

'Yes, unfortunately. We can get the property listed again as soon as possible. I'm sure there'll be interest,' she told me. This was at the start of the pandemic. We weren't yet wearing masks, but serious concern about what was to come had starting to creep in and people definitely weren't thinking about moving unless they had to.

I'm quite sure there won't be, I thought.

'Wonderful, thank you,' I replied.

In the first two weeks, a handful of people viewed the property. Two people applied. One didn't pass the application process, the second revoked their application soon after they'd submitted it. A third person inspected but didn't apply.

I called my bank and asked for a three-month mortgage pause. Another week passed, no takers. Suddenly, I realised the importance of diversifying my investments. A mortgage wasn't a strategy, it was everything I had, invested in one market, which had the potential to head south quickly, undoing everything I'd achieved.

I weighed up the options. I'd had my investment property for almost six and a half years. During that time its value had increased. But the economic outlook was uncertain. If I didn't sell now, I risked holding a property with no equity. Worse, it could decline in the future and become worth less than I owed.

I decided to sell.

In the past few years, I've spoken to several people who've made a tree change, opting out of the city in favour of a slower, more environmentally friendly lifestyle, and I've envied them. Now, I wonder if I can make enough to trade in my investment, climb onto the next rung of the property ladder and secure a regional home.

Can I become that woman in a wide-brim hat, trimming her rose bushes with secateurs and tending to her vegetable patch while waving at passing neighbours? If you'd asked thirty-year-old me if this was what I'd long for, the answer would have been a hard *no*. But the ageing process is gently having its way with me, and now, as I near forty, I dream of little else. And my desire to get out of the city has only been strengthened by the pandemic.

But if I am going to become Lady Nic of Regional Vic, I want to do it properly.

For some time I've tried to do my bit for the environment, but it's been a pitiful effort at best. I take a mug from home when I buy takeaway coffee at my local cafe. But how many emissions are produced in the making of my caffeine hit? And that's just one coffee, in one cafe. What about all the other cafes in my suburb, my city, the country, the world?

Add to that my love of almond-milk lattes. I choose almond milk for its many health benefits, but beekeepers argue that in California, the location that provides 80 per cent of the world's almond supply, the massive amounts of pesticides used are killing the bees that pollinate the almonds. A survey of commercial beekeepers indicated that 50 billion bees died during the northern winter of 2018/19 – just so those of us avoiding dairy could get our hipster coffee.

They're just bees, you might say. But actually, they're essential for food production. You want to keep eating? You need to give a shit about how human consumption is impacting the environment, and the bees.

Nate Donley, a senior scientist for the Center for Biological Diversity in the United States, told *The Guardian* in early 2020, 'It's like sending the bees to war. Many don't come back.'

Suddenly my almond-milk latte tastes incredibly bitter.

To have a zero-impact environmental footprint, I'd have to live off-grid, grow my own fruit and veg, and perhaps fashion my winter jumpers out of wool produced by the sheep living on my land. What would I do all day? I'd have to give up my computer and my smartphone and write using pen and paper – recycled paper, obviously. Naturally, I'd have to give up the coffee too.

I know, I'm being dramatic, but the point is I'm a walking contradiction. So many of us are. To live in modern society is to contribute to carbon emissions and environmental damage. I'm only one person, so creating meaningful change seems impossible. Plus, if I'm honest, I'm no Greta Thunberg. I drive a car almost every day and, with embarrassing frequency, I order Uber Eats meals that are wrapped in layers of future waste. I'm also a huge fan of air conditioning.

Which brings me to the problem that most average punters face. A problem I can't reconcile. I want to secure a comfortable financial future, live in a decent house and build an investment portfolio that protects me well into my retirement. I can't possibly claim to care about the planet's future when I'm simultaneously focused on getting rich or at least comfortable enough to eat more than gruel in a dodgy old folks' home when I'm on the downward slide, can I?

Also, there'll be no point in achieving financial freedom if there's no planet to live on. Ugh, are we screwed either way?

After mulling this over, I've decided it's perfectly acceptable to want to build wealth, particularly if it enables me to help my family and friends during a time of crisis. Once I've taken care of my own backyard, I can consider the neighbouring lawns, gardens, forests and oceans beyond my front fence.

I'm not perfect, and living in Australia – where the 2019–20 bushfires contributed to two-thirds of the nation's annual carbon emissions in a matter of weeks – means that I play a part in the climate crisis. I also have to accept that residing in this nation means working hard to get ahead. The cost of living is high, and I have to make money.

As I consider an idyllic sustainable life in a charming town, I think about the prospect of doing my bit for the bees, by keeping some of my own. I could potentially go off-grid and dramatically cut my personal emissions. But I know this is only one part of the equation. There's no point in doing all of this if my superannuation is invested in companies that promote fossil fuels or if I'm banking with one of the Big Four, which often profit from investing in similarly dubious ventures.

I can choose how I build my wealth. I can choose not to be a total arsehole about it. Perhaps I can even make money through ethical investment, so the next time a pandemic strikes, I can buy a stack of toilet paper and then hand it out to people who need it more than me.

And if I'm going to do this with a completely clear conscience, I want to 'greenify' all of my money. That's because I've spent several years looking into the possible future prosperity of my generation, and those who will follow us. I worry that not only are house prices astronomical, but our money is also inadvertently funding dying sectors, climate change and businesses that probably won't do us any good in the future.

So, in the coming chapters I'll research ethical super, banking, shares and other investment opportunities, and pass on what I learn to you. Here we are, all starting out together. By the end of this book I plan to have an ethical superannuation account, the beginnings of a respectable ethical share portfolio, cash stashed with a progressive bank and the knowledge required to build a fire-resistant, sustainable home.

In each case, I'll also be looking for the best possible investment return. I might not be able to make a big impact on my own, but if we all invest in good, we reduce the power of those putting up the roadblocks.

But first, it's important for me to point out that this is the financial process that I've chosen to go through. I'm going to look at as many options as possible so that you can get a broad understanding of what's out there. The things I invest in will be aligned with my values, my financial situation and my goals. Yours, naturally, will be different.

I'm not a financial adviser, economist, ethicist or climate scientist. I'm just a regular person, seeking to sort the dodgy options from the good ones. If I make mistakes I'll admit to them, so you can learn from my errors. Importantly, I know that there's an ethical spectrum. To find an investment that doesn't harm the environment or society in some way is exceedingly difficult. I am going to do my best, but as ethical investing is still in relative infancy, perfection is damn hard to come by. Still, seeking out sustainable options is better than not trying at all.

If what you read in the coming pages inspires you to get ethical, I suggest talking to your own financial adviser or trusted finance person in your life, so that you can take a holistic approach to your strategy. An early spoiler: it doesn't take me long to realise that there are a million shades of grey to wade through before you see the green light.

1

What Is Ethical Investment?

ETHICAL OR SOCIALLY RESPONSIBLE INVESTING involves consciously putting money into financial plans or businesses that don't damage the environment or have negative social outcomes. The aim, of course, is to simultaneously derive a return on that investment.

It turns out that ethical investment isn't a new concept. The Quakers were doing it back in the eighteenth century, insisting that their members couldn't engage slaves, arguing, rightly, that a trade that involved the buying and selling of people was immoral. Similarly, in the same era, Methodist preacher John Wesley wrote a sermon called *The Use of Money*. In it, he questions whether gold, silver and other valuables were to blame for corruption. 'The love of money, we know, is the root of all evil; but not the thing itself. The fault does not lie in the money, but in them that use it,' he concluded.

Man, this guy had no idea how much worse things were going to get.

By the twentieth century, more people were advocating against investing in 'sin stocks'. But, while a small number of people could see the benefit of investing in good over evil, the reality was that alcohol, tobacco, gambling and coal paid the big bucks.

Ethical investment funds started to pop up in Australia during the 1980s and 1990s. But it wasn't until the early 2000s that increasing consumer pressure and 'green activism' pushed those running larger institutions to sit up and take notice.

This wasn't just about climate change, though. The word 'ethical' is open for interpretation in the investment space. Being ethical in business means different things to different people. It also depends on what your business is. A beauty company might be considered ethical because its research and development doesn't involve testing on animals. An accounting firm might be considered ethical because it pays its staff above award wages and provides quality working conditions. A fashion designer might be considered ethical if they choose to manufacture their garments locally, create domestic jobs and advocate against child labour.

So, where are we at right now?

Today, according to the Responsible Investment Association Australasia (RIAA), approximately $1 trillion of the $2.24 trillion in managed funds is classified as 'responsible'. That's not just because Australians are increasingly more aware of the impact their investments can have, it's because ethical investment is really starting to pay. Big time.

A 2019 report by the RIAA showed that responsible share portfolios are consistently outperforming the benchmark. While the ASX 300 index showed returns of 5.6 per cent over five years and 8.91 per cent over ten years, ethical investment was returning 6.43 per cent and 12.39 per cent, respectively.

It's hardly a surprise. Ethical investment and innovation go hand-in-hand. Sustainable, environmentally friendly and socially conscious businesses are often making essential contributions to our future, and frequently taking a tech-focused approach. They provide products and services that are in demand. And where there's demand, there's likely going to be an ongoing return on investment.

Imagine if you'd invested in Google just as the internet was taking off. The same logic can be applied to your approach to ethical investment. Why *wouldn't* I invest in renewable energy over coal? It makes sense to put my money into healthcare rather than tobacco. Aged care is among the fastest-growing sectors in Australia, and the need for better services and facilities is going to impact all of us in the future.

But if you were an early adopter of Google shares, you were taking a massive risk. No one knew it was going to be the behemoth that it is today. There was no history of returns when Google first went public. So if you're investing in ethical ventures that are new, it's important to do research, as much as is possible, with whatever information is available.

Of course, we are seeing plenty of ethical disruptors that are delivering returns to happy shareholders. Like all shares, though, ethical options can rise and fall over time. Nonetheless, investors are keeping a very close eye on the ethical market.

Why green is the new black

There are a few reasons why ethical investment is on the up. For starters, young professionals are becoming acutely aware that they can invest in products that are aligned with their values, and that's driving a significant amount of change. Say what you will about smashed-avocado-eating millennials, but they're leading the charge. According to a 2017 survey by Lonergan Research on behalf of RIAA, millennials were the most likely cohort (75 per cent of respondents) to choose a super fund with environmental, social and governance screening, while also seeking to maximise their returns. Sixty-nine per cent said they would consider ethical investment in the future.

Secondly, the barrier to entering the ethical investment market is much lower than it once was. Take, for example, the advent of micro-investing apps and exchange traded funds (ETFs). ETFs are comprised of several shares and assets. They're bought and sold on the stock exchange, just like individual shares. The difference is you get to buy a bundle of shares in one trade. So rather than buying a single share of one company, you're buying a very small share of lots of companies or assets. A key benefit is the diversification of ETFs. While one company in your ETF might take a dip in value due to market activities, that doesn't mean they all will.

Micro-investing apps allow you to put spare change into your fund of choice. While $5 here or there might not seem like much, over time, as the dollars grow, so too does your ability to build a portfolio. Some of these apps don't charge fees at all until you reach a certain threshold, meaning you can experiment with little risk to begin with.

Through this investment type, budding investors are able to achieve broad exposure to ethical investments for a reasonable price. We'll talk about ETFs and micro-investing in more detail in the coming chapters.

And third, the sheer volume of people entering the market is giving ethical investment some explosive potential. In Australia, in particular, there's a growing awareness of the individual consumer's power to vote with their transactions.

Who's already ethically investing?

If you think ethical investing is just for daisy-chain-making, left-wing folks holding signs at climate-change rallies, think again. You don't have to be an outspoken social media keyboard warrior to be an ethical investor, either; there are plenty of wealthy, silent investors, speaking through those powerful dollar bills of theirs.

According to a *Harvard Business Review* article from June 2019, many business leaders and investment fund managers are quietly moving money into ethical spaces and, as a result, this has become seriously big business. After interviewing seventy senior executives at forty-three global investment firms, the article's authors, Robert G. Eccles and Svetlana Klimenko, found that most of their interviewees were heavily focused on ethical pursuits, not just because it was good for the world, but because it was good for their hip pockets too.

The article highlights the fact that when the UN-supported Principles for Responsible Investment (PRI) launched in 2006, sixty-three investment companies jumped on board, with a tidy US$6.5 trillion in assets under management. In April 2018, signatories spiked to a figure of 1715 and accounted for US$81.7 trillion in assets under management.

The authors argue, 'When it becomes clear that the people who decide whether to buy or sell a company's stock have internalized ESG [environmental, social and corporate governance] into their calculations, the business leaders will be forced to do the same within their companies.'

And that could have a massive impact on the collective consciousness.

Gone are the days where big companies get to avoid political and social issues. Businesses are increasingly realising that people's ethics will have an impact on their perception of the brand. Take Airbnb, for example. It's not a perfect company as its business model impacts people seeking long-term private rentals, but it is taking action on social issues. In 2017, during Donald Trump's controversial immigration ban, Airbnb launched a campaign offering free short-term housing to 100,000 refugees over the next five years. They even ran an ad during the Super Bowl – that's expensive media property – with the message

#WeAccept beamed into homes across the United States.

That said, it doesn't work if it's tokenistic. Ethical commitments that companies make have to be genuine, or they risk being called out for jumping on the bandwagon.

Increasingly, many of us want our purchases and investments to be responsible. *Australian Financial Review* reporter James Fernyhough pointed out in 2019 that almost half of professionally managed money in Australia is now classified as 'responsible investment'. He called this 'a meteoric rise for a sector that was still considered niche five years ago'.

'The Responsible Investment Association Australasia (RIAA) now classes 44 per cent – or nearly $1 trillion – of the $2.24 trillion managed by professional investors as "responsible",' he added.

But I suspect the reason that the word 'responsible' is in quote marks is because the concept of being responsible can be interpreted in so many ways. A company can be considered responsible if they have a woman on the board, even though the business is mining, which generates significant volumes of fossil fuels. They might pay above award wages but be a massive carbon emitter. They might have a corporate social responsibility philosophy – most big businesses do – but whether they walk the talk is a different matter entirely.

In short, 'responsible' is a really loose term, and it's up to us to tighten up the concept. Responsible and ethical screening is still murky to say the least, but as more people wake up to the way their money is invested, they'll inevitably help to refine the screens and call out the frauds.

That's where you come in.

How do I define what's ethical?

Before you can even think about ethical investment, you need to decide exactly what your ethics are. Your ethics may not be the same as mine. The morals that influence your choices will likely have been formed as a result of your upbringing, life experiences and, perhaps, political views.

According to Australia-based not-for-profit The Ethics Centre, you can create your ethical framework based on your values, principles and purpose:

- Values tell us what's good – they're the things we strive for, desire and seek to protect.

- Principles tell us what's right – outlining how we may or may not achieve our values.

- Purpose is your reason for being – it gives life to your values and principles.

I haven't spent much time thinking about the specifics of what's morally right or evil since my high school ethics classes. And, if memory serves, I wasn't particularly engaged in that. Broadly, I know there are things that I see as important for my future and the future of those around me. So I started to think about what my values are and what I feel is ethical and really questioning what I stand for. I've confirmed that I don't value investment in coalmining and that I want to see investment in better solutions for our future. *Any* solutions. For example, I want to eliminate direct and indirect investment in fossil fuels. But divesting from fossil fuels is not enough, I'd like to see Australia make epic strides towards renewable solutions. We have the know-how and the capacity to do it, so it's really just a matter of sourcing funding and implementing a strategy to shift out of coal and into renewables.

I'm also particularly interested in businesses that prioritise diversity of their boards – probably because I'm a woman who's seen talented colleagues walk away from careers because they didn't see a path to leadership. I also know that women do not have as much super or income as their male counterparts. In fact, the gap is a staggering 28 per cent. According to a report from consultancy KPMG, published in August 2021, men aged between sixty and sixty-four have a median super balance of $204,107, compared to women in the same bracket, who have $146,900.

Technology that powers cultural change is something I'm interested in too. I know that good tech has the potential to change our lives for the better.

I'm keen to learn more about companies that are focused on wellbeing, so that might involve green food technology – more sustainable approaches to food production, quality control and distribution, for example. Until recently, I haven't spent much time thinking about healthcare, but a pandemic tends to change your outlook. Suddenly, scientific research into medicine seems pretty damn important.

Something that's crucial to me is aged care and affordable housing. This is personal. I know far too many people who won't retire with a property portfolio. I've spoken to several women who are terrified about what their future holds because they don't own a home or have a share portfolio to deliver income beyond the pension and their superannuation balance is not enough. It's a massive problem in Australia and there's much work to be done as our population ages, so I'll be on the lookout for companies that are finding compelling solutions to these problems too.

But as I do my research, I'm coming to realise that my ethical focus should not just be on the industries I like, but also on the way companies conduct themselves. And it's not until I start moving my money around that I realise how much I value honesty, integrity and innovation.

Your criteria might be different. Perhaps you have a passion for Australian wildlife. Alternatively, you might be interested in sustainable fashion and companies that take a zero-tolerance approach to child labour practices in the making of your garments. It'll be up to you to look into ventures that speak to you. In doing that, you'll probably find that you're really compelled to do something about it.

That's part of the joy of ethical investing. It's not just chucking some cash into shares and watching your returns rise – you get the dual benefit of knowing that the businesses you put your valuable coin into will have better prospects of doing things you actually give a shit about and, in turn, may improve our future.

How do companies define what's ethical?

Unfortunately, there's no uniform indication of what constitutes 'ethical'. There's also no regulation to clarify what ethical investing is as a basic standard. So you need to navigate the marketing.

To give you an idea of how the big superannuation funds and ethical investment firms decide what's ethical and what's not, here's a list of the ways their investments might be screened. It's still not foolproof, but it's a start.

Negative screening
The negative screening process involves putting companies through assessments to find out if they're invested in things that people broadly deem unethical. If they produce an addictive product or service (tobacco, gambling), they're unlikely to get over the ethical hurdle. Likewise, if they engage in poor labour practices, they can be struck off the list of potential investment.

Negative screening is a good place to start when deciding what you will and won't invest in. If you are staunchly opposed to tobacco, obviously you won't want your investment portfolio to include a company that makes cigarettes.

Positive or 'best-in-class' screening

This involves seeking out companies that have good social and ethical values, such as a zero-carbon-emissions policy, a gender-diverse board and exemplary treatment of staff in the production of goods and services. In essence, they turn a profit by doing the right thing. Ideally, they do everything right, but depending on who's screening, they might only need to meet one or a handful of items in the criteria to make the cut.

Companies that perform well in a positive screening process often make a tangible difference to environmental or social outcomes. And, in a perfect world, they're a good investment too. This might include sectors such as healthcare, education and renewable energy.

Minimum standards or 'norms-based' screening

This approach uses the minimum standard of company, government or international standards. The minimum standards depend on which filter they're put through. So, for example, they may be subject to assessment based on the Ten Principles of the UN Global Compact. These principles are based, in part, on the Universal Declaration of Human Rights.

The principles cover topics such as:

- human rights (non-compliance in human rights abuses)

- labour (recognition of the right to collective bargaining and elimination of compulsory labour and child labour, elimination of discrimination)

- the environment (precautionary approaches to environmental concerns, environmental responsibility and the development of environmentally friendly technologies)

- anti-corruption.

Sustainability investing

This is a specific environmental approach, and it means actively seeking out funds or investment opportunities in clean-water programs, renewable energy, infrastructure, recycling, waste management and more.

Environmental, Social and Governance (ESG) investing

ESG covers environmental, social and governance screening principles. If this is the screen you're using, you might need to dig a bit to see just how good a company's governance is. These sweeping general areas make it possible for businesses to claim they're meeting the ESG criteria when, in fact, it's a regular business where people are paid the nominated award wages and there's a recycling bin next to the printer. Perhaps they report on sustainability during their annual general meeting, but potentially there's little real change being driven. That's not to say there aren't companies with a great commitment to ESG, but you need to be comfortable with where they sit on what is a massive spectrum.

Impact investing

If you choose impact investing as a key screen, you're ultimately looking to see physical results from your investment. That might come in the form of improved transport and infrastructure, schools or hospitals. Equally, the impact might be improved social outcomes locally or internationally. Either way, you'll seek to get a return on investment while hopefully being able to see an actual result.

Watch out for greenwashing

When it comes to choosing superannuation and shares, you need to be aware of 'greenwashing'. That's essentially where a company, super fund or organisation providing you with the opportunity to purchase their products and services, or invest in the business, will claim it's green when it's not at all, or not nearly as green as it's hyped to be. There is no industry regulation. Greenwashing is everywhere – from superannuation and banking to housing and shares – so you have to be really diligent when doing research.

The term greenwashing, which is also known as 'green sheen', was coined by New York environmentalist Jay Westerveld in 1986. He wrote a university essay about a hotel in Fiji that had put a cute little card on the bathroom vanity encouraging people to reuse their fluffy white towels, in an effort to reduce the environmental costs of washing and to minimise ecological damage. He suspected that, given the resort was expanding, with more bungalows under construction, the reduced frequency of towel washing would make little difference, although it created an illusion of care for the brand and, as a result, perhaps increased patronage and profit. 'It all comes out in the green-wash,' he wrote in the essay, which was later widely circulated.

At that time, big corporations were confident they were above any scrutiny of greenwashing practices. Take oil company Chevron. In the mid-1980s, the company made several fancy commercials, played on television and published in newspapers, to highlight its caring corporate citizen ethos. These ads were actually a thinly veiled attempt to justify exploration for oil. In one example, a bear is shown asleep on the land and the voice over explains that Chevron does its work without interrupting the grizzly's winter hibernation. It's narrated like a bedtime story:

People with motors and machinery will explore for oil through deep winter, but before she wakes the people will be gone. The explored land will be replanted so it will soon look as if no one had ever been there. The people sometimes work all through the winter, so nature can have spring all to herself.

So considerate of you, large oil drilling company.

Even better was oil company DuPont's 1991 commercial where the voice-over guy claims: 'Recently DuPont announced that its energy unit Conoco would pioneer the use of new double-hulled oil tankers in order to safeguard the environment.'

At the end of the thirty-second spot, seals clap enthusiastically and a dolphin jumps for joy.

You couldn't make this shit up.

At first, I thought, *Well, it was the 1980s and '90s.* But a bit more research shows this is still very much happening.

In 2019, Nestle USA was faced with a class-action lawsuit after allegedly labelling its products with claims that its cocoa beans were 'sustainably sourced'. In fact, the plaintiffs argued that the cocoa was coming from farms that used child labour, while also using production processes that polluted waterways and killed wildlife. Despite that, the federal judge ultimately dismissed the lawsuits, saying that while the use of child and slave labour practices was 'beyond dispute', the consumers failed to show exactly how the company had deceived them.

Confounding as that judgement is, the lawsuit emphasises that consumers are far more aware than they once were and they're making noise about greenwashing.

Where do I start?

If you think the idea of getting into investment is overwhelming, you're not alone. On a one to ten scale of investment knowledge, where one is a bin chicken digging for shiny coins and ten is a stockbroker in a sharp suit, I am probably a two. And I only give myself the step up from bin chicken because I understand the process of buying a house.

So, just like you, I'm starting out. I'm sharing what I learn, as I get the info. Here are some of the options I intend to explore:

Shares and exchange traded funds (ETFs)

I've never bought a share or an ETF in my life. I have no idea how to start a share portfolio. An ETF is a type of security that tracks an index sector, commodity or asset. An index typically measures the performance of a particular sector. So, for example, it might mirror tech, sustainability or health industries. But rather than buying one share in one company, you buy a very small share of many companies, focused on a specific theme.

In the coming chapters, I'll highlight the ways in which I've slowly been gaining an understanding of ethical shares and ETFs, without investing too much while I'm learning. I know that to buy shares or ETFs, I need to choose what's called a brokerage platform – that's where I purchase the items that I want to invest in. I need to understand the fees associated with each option, the pros and cons of using each platform and, importantly for me, the ethical drivers behind the share or the ETF. I quickly learn that ETFs can be trickier to assess when it comes to ethical investment, because I'm not just considering the ethics of one individual company, I need to think about every single company or asset that makes up the contents of the ETF.

Superannuation

To say I have been ambivalent about my superannuation is an understatement. Until a few years ago I had about six super accounts. I'd just open a new account every time I started a new job – whichever provider my employer used – and then forget about it. I rolled it all into one account after someone told me how much money I was losing in fees. It took about two minutes to get this done in my myGov account. I should have done that painfully simple piece of life admin much sooner.

Many Australians don't give much thought to their superannuation but the reality is, if you have a super account, you're an investor. The money you contribute is invested so that your nest egg grows over time. The reason I hadn't cared about it was because I couldn't touch it for another couple of decades … so, whatever. But, actually, being a bit more proactive could make a big difference down the track. Plus, I don't even know what my money contributes to. Could be military-grade weapons for all I know. I really should look into that if I'm going to become an ethical investor.

Banking

A bank is a bank – they're all the same, right? Wrong. Let's say you have $5000 in your savings account. The bank makes money from fees and charges along with the interest it earns, which is then lent out to others, who invest that money in other ventures. So your humble savings might be contributing to things that you don't support. Do you want your money going towards the expansion of coalmines? If you don't, you might want to do some research into what your bank invests in.

Sustainable housing

It's not just the complex world of shares and super that I'll look into. Property is often the biggest investment many of us will take on. I'd like my next property to at least have some sustainable components. I wonder if it's possible to build a sustainable home that will deliver long-term returns, both in value and through minimal running costs.

I hope to buy a shack in a regional town, but as Australia faces the ongoing threat of devastating bushfires thanks to climate change, there are inherent risks. How do I choose a location that makes sense from an investment perspective while also being safe from fire? Is that even a possibility anymore? It's never been more important to build with fireproof materials. How much will that set me back? If the cost of the build results in overcapitalising, is it worth it?

It's no secret that Australians love property, but it's getting increasingly difficult for young buyers to obtain. Banks continue to profit, and the construction industry is responsible for considerable carbon emissions. Is it even possible to buy or build ethically? We'll soon find out.

Ethical admin checklist

 Establish your ethics. Think about your values and the sectors that are aligned with these values.

 What is non-negotiable for you? What is acceptable?

 Consider ethical screens. Is the minimum standard enough for you or do you want investments that are considered 'best in class'?

 Understand greenwashing. Just because an investment product is labelled 'ethical' doesn't mean it will be aligned with your ethics. Do your research before committing.

 Choose your investment. Many of us have compulsory superannuation, but would you also like to start a share portfolio? Think about how much money you have available to invest and take some time to consider how you'd like to invest it.

2

How to Become a Super Hero

IN MY FIRST JOB, as a waitress, I filled out a form indicating I was happy for my superannuation contributions to go into the fund suggested by the human resources department. I didn't know a thing about super. All I knew was that money was swiftly captured on pay day and transferred to a place where I couldn't touch it for a *long* time. I was already slugging it out for minimum wage: taking orders, serving food, dealing with belligerent customers, making coffee and mopping the floors at the end of the night. If anything, I resented the fact that this money, which was rightfully mine, couldn't be spent on whatever whim I had at the time.

My indifference towards super continued into my professional life – I'd just tick the box that gave my employer permission to put my super into the default fund. In my twenties, I worked many freelance and contract jobs, so the little sums occupying each superannuation fund seemed to make little difference.

Eventually, I discovered that it wasn't actually that hard to provide the account number for my chosen fund when I started a new job, and to keep accumulating money in one place. When it came time to roll everything into one account, I wasn't particularly interested in choosing the one with the lowest fees, the best returns or an ethical investment strategy. At the time, I was working for a large, respected media organisation and I assumed that their choice of fund was somehow superior to the ones on offer in my previous roles. It also had the most money in it. Click, click, done.

Up until a few years ago, I didn't stop to think about how superannuation worked. I had no idea that my money was reinvested in other businesses so that my super would grow through the returns derived from those investments. Once I discovered this was the case, I thought, *Oh yeah, that makes sense*. Then I went back to watching Netflix or scrolling through Instagram.

I vaguely understood that my money was invested in things like shopping centres, infrastructure and shares. It never occurred to me that it might be invested in sinister stuff.

How superannuation actually works

Superannuation is a compulsory system of placing a minimum percentage of your income into a fund to support your financial needs in retirement. It's invested in all sorts of assets so that the lump sum grows over time. But you generally can't access it until you're in your sixties. That changed when the federal government granted access to superannuation during Covid-19. Of course, many people were experiencing financial hardship during this time and needed cash fast. Others were simply raiding their retirement piggy bank to splash out on new cars and botox.

This was, arguably, a terrible long-term decision. More than a million Australians applied for early access to up to $20,000 in tax-free super. Dipping into those funds early can have a serious impact at retirement. Worryingly, young people under thirty-five made up a significant chunk of those withdrawals. If you accessed yours, it could be a good idea to make additional contributions if you're able to, so that you can get your balance back up. 'Future you' will appreciate it.

As boring as super might be, it's really important. We have an ageing population, so relying on the aged pension is set to become increasingly difficult. That's not to say you should rely on your super-annuation alone – it will ideally be just one part of your wealth-building strategy – but because it's locked away, you can't lose your super nest egg through a dodgy investment or impulsive spending.

In most cases, if you as an employee earn $450 or more before tax in a month, your employer needs to contribute to your super fund. The figure is currently 10 per cent of your salary and it should be paid into your account quarterly. It will continue to rise incrementally from 2022.

Your super is invested in a range of assets to help grow your balance so you can have the best possible retirement outcome. That's all pretty straightforward, but what you mightn't be aware of is the complexities behind the scenes. When your money is reinvested, it could be going into cash, shares or bonds. Generally, once you've nominated your fund, you probably don't dive too deep into what the investments are – because as long as you're getting a return, does it matter?

Well, yeah, it does if you want to invest ethically.

The admin begins

Now, imagine there's an invisible label on every super account that says: *May contain traces of fossil fuels, pornography, alcohol and gambling*. Would you buy a product with that label? I wouldn't. But again, that's just where my ethics lie. I should note, however, that there are forms of ethical pornography out there. Perhaps you like a flutter on horseracing, in which case gambling might not be a total deal-breaker for you. This is all deeply personal.

Employers need to provide you with a super fund option when you start a new job. These funds are an Australian Tax Office requirement and they're designed to be simple, diversified products with low fees. Ethical considerations are often not a primary focus.

It was time for me to do some painful admin work and find out how my humble sum of super savings was being used.

So for the first time, in January 2020, I log into my fund to see what my money is contributing to. Curiously, I find absolutely nothing specific. The dashboard is pretty sophisticated. It highlights my account balance and a projected figure that I might have by retirement age that's based on my contributions to date. My current investments are apparently 'very confident', which would be more reassuring if I knew exactly what my current investments are.

When I click through to the investment section, I'm given the opportunity to view my unit holdings. I can also click 'edit' to make changes. I'm invested in a generic product designed for a group for people born between 1973 and 1983. Apparently, my age dictates how aggressive my investment strategy can be. 'You have many years left to retirement and time to see through the ups and downs of a more aggressive investment approach, so your money is invested in mainly growth assets,' reads the description.

I select 'asset allocation' so I can finally understand precisely how my cash is distributed. The breakdown includes growth investments, defensive investments, Australian shares, international shares, real assets, alternative assets, growth fixed interest, defensive fixed interest and cash. The reason I'm working hard to find the specific list of holdings is because it allows me to see all the individual companies my money is invested in. Alternative assets sound questionable. And what the hell is defensive fixed interest? All in all, this means absolutely nothing to me.

There's a pie chart that indicates 85 per cent of my money has been invested in growth assets (which includes shares and property). The document says these have the potential to grow in value over time. Great. The remaining 15 per cent is invested in defensive assets (fixed interest and cash), which provide investors with less volatility in the shorter term. Also great. I think?

I download statements and search every possible section trying to find any sign of a specific investment. Alas, there's nothing. So I send off a couple of emails asking to speak to someone to obtain a list of actual companies that I'm ignorantly helping to fund.

The following day I get an auto-generated reply that tells me how to click through to the investment section of my portfolio and see how my money is invested (I already did that). While the section outlines a range of investment types, it doesn't name any business specifically that I'm invested in.

There's also a booklet with more information attached to the email detailing the investment types: Australian shares, international shares, real assets (property and infrastructure), alternative assets (hedge funds, private equity), growth fixed interest, defensive fixed interest and cash.

Eventually, I speak to a human and I'm told I can have a phone meeting with one of the company's financial advisers in a week's time. So I wait, and conduct research into alternatives in the meantime, although if I'm honest they've already lost me as a customer. Any company that's investing my money and can't tell me where it's placed within a day or two of my enquiry is not one I want to do business with. This information should be provided up-front when people join superannuation funds, or at least listed transparently on their website. This is my money, and your money. We should have the right to know where it's invested.

To be fair, investing in the share market is incredibly complex and fund managers are constantly changing the investment mix in line with what's happening in the economy. But surely someone can give me at least a broad view of my investment composition? All those years of superannuation apathy are catching up with me, but I'm excited to make up for lost time.

A week later, I speak to an adviser. As soon as I explain that I'm looking for a list of holdings that my super is invested in, I'm told, 'That's something I wouldn't have access to.'

You've got to be kidding me, mate.

The guy puts me on hold and comes back to me a few minutes later, explaining that he has the most recent quarterly report, which has some, but not all of the information.

When I ask why I'm still not able to get something concrete, he tells me that my account has a multi-manager setup, and those investment managers, shifting my money around as they please, have their own 'secret recipe' for how it's invested. 'They don't want to expose that to competitors,' he adds slowly. Obviously, I can't see him, but I'm pretty sure he's sweating, seeing he's clearly hesitating before uttering every word. But then he goes on to tell me my plan is what's called a 'ready-made' option. If it's ready-made, I can't understand why it's so hard to give me a list of holdings and I politely query this, to no avail.

It's clear that I'm not going to get what I'm looking for during this exchange. If I want more information, the adviser has to lodge a request with the administration team, so I ask him to do that. In the meantime, he sends me the quarterly report. 'It's a bit of a broad stroke. I'm not going to guarantee you'll get something rock solid,' he admits.

More information from the administrative team will arrive in three to five days, I'm assured. 'If that's not adequate you can follow up with the helpline,' he concludes. I thought he was the helpline. Apparently not.

When we end our call, I open the document, which is jammed with numbers and jargon but little clear information. It does, however, outline my 'top ten' Australian share holdings. The list reveals that I'm investing in several major mining companies and Australian banks that I know invest heavily in activities that contribute to fossil fuels.

From an ethical standpoint, this doesn't even come close to something I can be proud of, so I start looking for a fund that invests in businesses that I can confidently say I believe in.

Campaigning for change

I thought the contents of my superannuation were bad, but I wasn't nearly as shell-shocked as Dr Bronwyn King was when she found out what her money was invested in. Working as an oncologist at the lung cancer unit of the Peter MacCallum Cancer Centre in Melbourne, she was exposed to the devastating impact that smoking can have on individuals and their families.

Sitting with a superannuation representative in the Peter MacCallum cafe, some years into her career, she learned that her own savings were invested in the very thing that she was working so hard against: tobacco. 'I was just flattened by it. It made me feel like everything I was doing up until that point, trying to help people suffering as a result of tobacco use, was being completely undermined by my own money,' Dr King tells me.

For those who develop lung cancer, the outcomes are poor. On hundreds of occasions she'd seen patients die and counselled their families through the experience. 'There was this sense of total futility. What is the point? Here I am going to work every day, totally aware of the brutal impact. To think that I was investing in the companies that made the products causing that suffering, it just made no sense.'

That meeting would completely change her career path. 'The realisation at the cafe at Peter McCallum – that was the moment. There was this strong sense that I wasn't going to let that go,' Dr King says.

And she didn't. Shortly after that meeting, she started Tobacco Free Portfolios, a not-for-profit organisation designed to work with financial institutions to stop investment in and financing of tobacco. Eight years later, Dr King and her small team are responsible for getting tobacco out of more than 15 million Australian superannuation funds.

She has set the gold standard in making a difference in the ethical and sustainable investment space. Her breakthrough moment was receiving approval to launch her flagship initiative, the Tobacco-Free Finance Pledge, at the United Nations in New York in September 2018.

Now, this is not something your average punter can just do. To hold one of these formal events you need sign-off from at least two prime ministers or presidents. Malcom Turnbull, who was in office at the time, got on board.

'Six weeks later I opened a letter at my house – it had been sitting in a pile on my desk for at least three days – and it was from the French president, Macron.'

'I guess we're going to the UN then,' she told her family. The Pledge was launched in partnership with the UN-supported Principles for Responsible Investment, the UN Environment's Principles for Sustainable Insurance, the UN Environment Programme Finance Initiative and financial partners including BNP Paribas, AXA, Natixis and AMP Capital. Today, there are 164 signatories worldwide, with a total of US$11 trillion dollars in assets under management signed up to the tobacco-free pledge shifted away from the tobacco industry.

Getting tobacco out of superannuation funds is clearly aligned with Dr King's career purpose. She tells me that about eight million people die from tobacco-related illnesses each year; according to the World Health Organization, there will be one billion deaths this century. 'The numbers are extraordinary,' she says.

Dr King understands, though, that this is just scratching the surface of a much bigger investment challenge. 'Early on I spoke to financial institutions about tobacco in the broader context of ethical and sustainable investment,' she says, and points out that tobacco is one of the easier challenges to deal with. 'You're in or you're out,' she adds.

But Dr King is all too aware that many sectors are so much more complex, and she reels off a list of those that remain an issue: 'Guns, pornography, gambling, sugar, human rights abuses, gender inequities, executive compensation, palm oil and every aspect of climate change'.

'What is important is to develop a sustainable investment framework that matches the issue with the appropriate tools that financial institutions have,' she explains. By contrast, she says, fossil fuels come with a broad set of challenges for financial institutions. 'The world needs energy. We need to transition from black or brown energy to green energy. We need to transition faster. I think the finance sector globally has become very aware of that need, but it's much more complex than just applying exclusions.'

Despite the impressive work Dr King has done so far, she indicates there is still much to be done. In 2013, the federal government released a public consultation and discussion paper called *Better Regulation and Governance, Enhanced Transparency and Improved Competition in Super- annuation*. The paper was designed to source feedback from companies and individuals regarding the state of transparency in the superannuation industry. Ideally, the result would have been improved regulation and legislation. Unfortunately, here we are almost a decade later and there's been little change.

Dr King was one of the many who made a submission. In terms of revealing people's holdings, she points out that some small funds don't have the resources to be updating their lists of holdings. However, she adds, some funds have adopted a form of disclosure. 'It shouldn't be that difficult to find out where your money is invested,' she says.

She is pursuing a relentless task, and even she has her moments when it comes to staying motivated. In 2019, Dr King found herself feeling incredibly burnt out. She was running Tobacco Free Portfolios full-time, while also continuing to run her own small oncology practice. 'I hit the wall, I took some time off and had a break from email,' she recalls.

During her week away she noticed a missed message from the director-general of the World Health Organization. He said, 'I wanted to thank you, it means a lot to us, we really think of you as a great partner in this work.'

Dr King says his appreciation was just what she needed to spur her on. 'It was the most perfect thing to say to someone who's burnt out. I needed something to lift the spirits. It meant an awful lot to me.' And so she continues her fight. 'I won't stop until the job is done. The time is now,' she concludes. In 2019, Dr King was honoured as Melburnian of the Year. The accolades continue to flow.

After hearing this story, I decided that believing that one person can't make a difference is just wrong, and I set my sights on doing my bit.

The rise of ethical investment specialists

Before I move my super, I make a call to Hope Evans, a financial adviser specialising in ethical investment. Since I bought my home, I've learned that personal finance doesn't operate in silos. It's all woven together. Move one wrong digit to a precarious place at an inopportune time and it can impact other parts of your wealth-building strategy, so it pays to check in with a professional, especially if you're exploring shares for the first time.

Hope was a proud Byron Bay local long before its streets were populated with designer boutiques and cafes selling fancy single-origin coffee and overpriced green smoothies. In the Byron of her youth, it was a true hippie town. Investors hadn't even contemplated snapping up properties to list on Airbnb, and Chris Hemsworth hadn't yet landed his role on *Home and Away*, let alone imagined a life in which he could afford one of the region's most palatial homes, located in an elevated setting overlooking Seven Mile Beach.

In the pre-Hemsworth era, Hope lived with her parents, who delivered doom-and-gloom messages about the planet's future. 'You guys are crazy, the world's not that bad,' she recalls thinking. So she set her mind to a traditional career, studying business and going on to work in financial planning. However, it didn't take long for Hope to get tangled in a web of unethical investment.

'I was arguing with my senior advisers when there was an oil spill in the Gulf of Mexico. I said, "We can't keep investing in things like this,"' she remembers. That incident, known as the Deepwater Horizon oil spill, occurred in April 2010, about 66 kilometres off the coast of Louisiana. The rig was owned by offshore oil-drilling company Transocean, and leased by BP. It's the worst oil spill in US history. Not only did it kill eleven people, according to US government officials, the leak was said to have peaked at approximately 60,000 barrels of oil per day. According to *The New York Times,* it's estimated that a total of 4.9 million barrels of oil had leaked – most of it into the gulf. A response team managed to collect or burn about 810,000 barrels before it reached the water.

Nonetheless, Hope's senior advisers saw no issue with continuing to invest their clients' hard-earned funds in such a venture. There were still good returns to be derived from companies like BP. So, like, what was her problem?

Not content to remain silent, Hope went on to study sustainable development and, shortly after, she combined this qualification with her business nous and started her own independent advisory.

Hope is no lone wolf in this burgeoning industry. Search the Ethical Advisers' Co-op website (ethicaladviserscoop.org) and you'll find ethical advisers all over the country, because the quality of ethical products varies dramatically. A novice like me, who wants to do the right thing but has no idea how, can benefit greatly. There are plenty of advisers who've gone into this area, which was considered niche just a few years ago, and now have a stack of people on their books.

An initial conversation with an ethical adviser is a good idea for so many reasons. It will quite often be free, which gives you a good chance to shop around. You want your adviser to understand your objectives. They might also give you some handy info that doesn't cost you a cent.

Hope sends me a heap of forms to fill out, in which I outline my current savings, mortgage, car repayments, credit-card debt, super-annuation and existing shares (currently zilch). Once she's assessed my position, she'll be able to contemplate my investment strategy and risk profile. It was a good exercise in that it forced me to look at the money coming in, my outgoings, my current investments and my savings.

I'm acutely aware of my capacity to get sucked in by flashy market-ing and the lure of cold hard cash. I need someone in my corner who knows the ethical sector better than I do. Someone who can help to protect my existing savings and help me grow it. I want to be ethical, but I don't want to put my money into ventures that are potentially going to lose money, of course.

Counting the cost of financial advice

It's a Tuesday afternoon and I'm sitting on my back deck tapping away at my laptop. Why aren't I at work? Well, I am at work. I have a flex-ible work arrangement and this was an important life choice I made for myself a few years ago. Now, thanks to Covid, many of us have the luxury of working on the couch, on our decks or balconies. But there's a big difference between being a freelancer, contractor or casual and having a full-time role – at least as far as the bank is concerned.

Prior to going freelance, I'd been working long hours in an advertising agency. Admittedly I was making a good living, but I was unfulfilled due to the toll it took on my lifestyle and the limitations of the work itself. I simply didn't believe in working on large campaigns for insurance companies, pharmaceutical firms and car brands.

Up until this point I'd worked hard to get ahead financially. I'd secured an investment property and I had some savings, which enabled me to take the leap into a world that provided so much more satisfaction. It made me a better person to be around and reignited my creativity.

But this was always going to have an impact on my opportunities to get comprehensive financial advice. Some people might be in a position to start with a lump sum and add to that figure consistently each month. My income fluctuates. At this moment, I don't have a huge amount to invest. I'm planning to start with a figure of $1000.

So when Hope comes back to me after running the numbers based on my circumstances, she points out that some people who have a managed portfolio might start with investing a figure such as $20,000 and then add $200 per month from their wage. I know that's not an option for me.

'You do not have a lot to invest at the moment. I can give you upfront or initial advice and then let you manage the portfolio ongoing yourself as my fees would be too high for a small portfolio,' she explains.

I'm a bit disheartened, but not exactly surprised. I know that most financial advisers charge a flat rate of anywhere between $1000 and $3000 for a complete financial plan, as well as a fee for ongoing portfolio management. It was nice to hear that she wasn't going to take advantage of me, though.

Essentially, you don't want your fees to counteract the value of your investment, so if you're starting small, you will likely want to keep your fees to a minimum too. In my case, this means I'm going to have to do my own work and speak to a range of people to establish my initial plans. I will perhaps return to Hope in time when I have more to invest. If you're like me and don't want to fork out a lot in fees for comprehensive consultations, you can talk to other people. An accountant might be a more affordable start. Alternatively, tax agents and your super provider could be in a position to provide guidance. But, as with anything, you get what you pay for. I do my best to seek out independent and trusted advice, sometimes from more than one source, before I make a decision about where my money goes. Sometimes, companies can have reasons for recommending particular financial products – reasons that benefit them. It really is worth doing a lot of research before making any commitments.

As part of our initial discussion, Hope is still able to give me some key things to consider as I look to move my super. I've found out that it's actually pretty easy to switch superannuation providers once I've chosen an alternative. But she urges me to consider the life insurance that might be built into my superannuation before I make the leap. 'When you move funds, you lose your life insurance,' she tells me, so I make a note to check that before I switch.

It turns out I had some incredibly basic cover included in my super, and I arranged more comprehensive cover with another provider when I bought my apartment – and I'm pretty comfortable with that, but it's good to know that I need to check for additional insurance charges when I set myself up with a new fund.

Soggy savings

Remember greenwashing? Well, it's particularly rife in the superannuation sector. In February 2020, *The Age* and *The Sydney Morning Herald* reported that four of Australia's largest industry super funds had invested billions of Australian workers' savings into coal production and other fossil fuel ventures, even though they were loud and proud about climate change. One of the worst offenders, UniSuper, had $7.82 billion invested in gas, oil and petrol companies.

In the company's November 2020 report, *Climate Risk and Our Investments*, UniSuper does admit that 'climate change and the transition to a low carbon economy will pose investment-related risk'. But in the following pages it highlights priorities including climate resilience, renewable energy, energy storage and a reduction in emissions. Hard to see how they'll achieve that as long as they remain heavily invested in fossil fuels.

The general party line for large superannuation funds is that by staying invested they're able to influence change. That, dear friends, is a bit of a cop-out. The reality is, it's going to be really hard for them to pull such large sums out of these companies without significant financial repercussions. But they know consumers are waking up to this, so they're doing their darndest to convince you that they're concerned about climate change.

Further down the rabbit hole, I find that even some companies using words such as 'ethical', 'sustainable' and 'green' in their brand names will apply sneaky layers to their offerings, so while they might have some good investment options, the nasties are tucked underneath, the idea being that they're buried too low for you to find them. According to Hope, many companies will say, '"Look at our sustainable options," but if you drill down, they'll still have the big miners and the big banks'.

A decent ethical super company will be doing comprehensive screening for greenwashing, but like I said, what you view as ethical might differ from the super company you're considering joining, so it can pay to do your own deep dive into the holdings you're thinking of putting your money into.

Now, armed with this information, I feel like I'm reviewing my superannuation options with my eyes wide open, and I turn my attention to finding an ethical super fund that's truly doing some good stuff.

Ethical admin checklist

 Consolidate your super. This means checking to see if you have more than one superannuation account. You can do this quickly and easily using the myGov website. Then select one account to put your funds into, and close the rest.

 Find out what's in your portfolio. Does your provider publish all of the holdings on its website? If not, give them a call. If they can't tell you, you need to decide if that's good enough.

 Consider more ethical alternatives. Do some research into the ethical funds available to you and see if you can find one that's aligned with your values.

 Speak to an independent professional. If you're unsure about what's right for you, it can pay to talk to a financial adviser (even if it's just an initial consultation) or accountant before making a decision.

3

Super Stars

IT TURNS OUT THERE ARE many companies focused on helping people achieve their ethical superannuation goals. I want to explore a range of companies I've heard about, including Australian Ethical, Future Super and Verve Super. Because I'm now aware of greenwashing, I arrange to talk to a few people who've already moved their super to see what their experience has been and to get some advice.

Melbourne-based Michael Poland is a committed climate activist. He has worked on a number of climate campaigns and is committed to mobilising people and their collective consumer power to switch to ethical options and increase the pressure on large institutions to clean up their investments. This includes campaigns for switching their energy companies to a renewable energy retailer, and to put pressure on banks not to invest in the Adani coalmine. 'These were very impactful – especially on Adani, which resulted in banks ruling out funding the project – which made me start to look at what other forms of divestment would be powerful', he says.

Michael likes Future Super and Verve Super. He ultimately moved his retirement nest egg over to Future Super because he'd dealt directly with the team and agreed with their approach. 'They're the most vocal super fund speaking out against funding fossil fuels, which I think is crucial. They work with a lot of climate campaigning groups and are really investing in ethical, positive change,' he says.

He points out that while moving away from a range of poor investment choices is great, reducing institutional fossil fuel funding is his top priority. 'In the next ten years we will see a huge amount of decarbonisation, including a shift away from fossil fuels. Having people help fast-track this transition will be crucial,' he suggests.

The future of super

On the back of Michael's advocacy, I look into Future Super. I go straight to the top and call founder Adam Verwey to find out about their super options.

Adam grew up in Broken Hill, a historic mining town in outback New South Wales. I've never been but Adam paints the picture, explaining that the mine is on the main street. 'If you're at a cafe having a coffee, you're looking onto the mine,' he says, and recalls the waste and the impact that left on him from childhood. He recalls the lead tailings – that's the materials left over after separating what's valuable. 'They pile it up into a hill,' Adam says.

It wasn't unusual for Adam's classmates to become seriously ill as a result of the environment they lived in. For those born in Broken Hill, growing up with high levels of lead in their systems was par for the course. As he got older, Adam learnt that the 'BH' in BHP stands for Broken Hill – the 'P' is for Propriety. The company derived its name from the silver and zinc mine that cast a shadow over Adam's innocent youth.

By the time he was in high school, Adam had a very clear picture of the reality. 'Kids were getting poisoned while shareholders got wealthy. I had nowhere to place this anger,' he says.

After graduating, he headed straight to university in Canberra and joined the student unions. It was there, in about 2002, that a conversation about how money was invested would come up. Adam looked into his modest superannuation account, which was with REST at that point, and found that 'BHP was right at the top'.

Back then, the only suitable alternative fund he could find was Australian Ethical. As fate would have it, it had an office across the road from his campus. He went into the office and moved his super over and applied for a job while he was at it, landing a role shortly after. He says it was an exciting time because it was so 'grassroots'.

'The founders were still in the business – they had a background in permaculture,' he laughs. I can't say I'd be in a hurry to hand my money over to people whose expertise is in gardening, but Adam says they were passionate and had engaged the right people to build the fund. When he started, it had $200 million in super funds; by the time he left, nine years later, it had reached $1 billion.

Despite that, Adam says that in 2013, when he was looking to make his next step, just 1 per cent of all super was labelled as ethical or sustainable, and he wanted to do more. But what about that billion over at Australian Ethical, you ask? It might sound like a lot, but today Australia has $3 trillion of Aussie citizens' money invested in superannuation. *Three trillion*. That's three thousand billion. So the humble billion over at Australian Ethical was spare change.

'I put my hand up to run in the federal election,' Adam says. Although he was 'one of those greens who knew they wouldn't win', he hoped the campaign would give him the opportunity to speak to more people about ethical super. Adam spent countless hours making phone calls, doorknocking and engaging with constituents. 'Maybe this is what we need to bridge that gap between the amount of people who say they want to switch and those who do,' he remembers thinking.

During this time, he met Simon Sheikh, the former head of activist group GetUp, who got close to winning a seat in the Senate. Adam and Simon talked a great deal about what could be done to 'bypass the political process' and drive change. The upside of Simon failing to win his seat was that he was 'excited and available', Adam recalls.

It took them nine months to get the funds set up and they launched Future Super in September 2014. The aim is not only to provide super funds that don't invest in fossil fuels, but simultaneously to build the finance required to invest in clean energy.

The team believes not just in moving away from fossil fuels but in taking a 'holistically ethical' approach too. That means they're invested in companies with strong social and environmental positions, as well as those that work to increase human wellbeing.

In 2018, Future Super released a report, *Supercharging Australia's Clean Energy Transition*. It was produced in conjunction with the Institute for Sustainable Futures at Sydney's University of Technology. The economic modelling suggests that with just 7.7 per cent of super funds invested between now and 2030, the power sector could be made 100 per cent renewable – '7.7 per cent could fund an entire clean energy grid. It shows the huge potential of what's in our super,' Adam says. The report also suggests that while absolute decarbonisation of the economy is a larger challenge, 12.4 per cent of funds invested between 2020 and 2050 could actually be enough to pull it off.

Plus, Adam reckons we're likely to have about $6 trillion to play with by 2035. With that sort of cash, we should be able to make a *Jetsons*-style transition to electric flying vehicles while we're at it.

But it might not happen if more people don't move their super to ethical funds.

Choosing your fund

If you're looking to switch to an ethical superannuation fund, you're probably interested in understanding how these companies put their super products together.

At Future Super, for example, positive and negative screens are used to establish the kinds of companies it includes in its portfolios. In the negative screening process, they work to remove fossil fuels, gambling, tobacco, weapons, slave labour, environmental destruction and more.

On the flip side, when choosing companies that might make the cut, they're looking for businesses focused on renewables, recycling, water conservation, healthcare, fair trade, social enterprise and ethical treatment of people and animals, to name a few.

Future Super provides three options for people who want to go ethical:

1. The Balanced Index is the lowest impact option. It ensures your super is free from fossil fuels but doesn't actively invest in positive ethical outcomes. 'The Balanced Index is for people who are more fee conscious,' Adam tells me, because the fees are lower, but says not many people choose this option. Nonetheless, they wanted to provide it to prospective customers.

2. Renewables Plus Growth, as the name suggests, is fossil-fuel-free, and invests approximately 20 per cent of the portfolio in renewable projects. This is the product that about 70 per cent of Future Super's customers choose.

3. Balanced Impact option has a broader ethical list. It's fossil-fuel-free and aims to increase a broad range of social and ethical outcomes (not just climate-focused initiatives).

Unlike my current provider, Future Super's full list of holdings is available on its website in a matter of clicks. They invest in some indisputably excellent ventures, including Meridian Energy, Australasia's largest 100 per cent renewable energy generator, and Infradebt, a company that helps to fund small renewable energy projects, such as hospitals and organisations that want to have a positive social impact. The list of holdings also includes American electric-car icon Tesla and entertainment streaming service Netflix.

But there's one thing I have to query with Adam. One organisation, Marsh & McLennan Companies, catches my attention. I know that this is a massive company responsible for insurance, risk management and a bunch of other financial services. It's also the parent company of my current superannuation company.

Adam says this is an example of where screening is complex. Marsh & McLennan gets through a negative screen because the core of the business is 'ethically neutral or mildly positive', Adam explains. 'These are really large companies and they're not going to be perfect,' he adds.

That said, Adam's on the front foot. In March 2020, it became clear that Marsh came under fire for its work arranging insurance for parts of the Adani coalmine project, while other insurers declined to support it.

'We are engaging with Marsh & McLennan, there's a good chance we won't hold that company soon,' Adam says.

It's not my intention to trip Adam up – I don't think this bloke who's spent his career campaigning for people to move their super over to ethical companies is actually out to invest in the very projects he's staunchly opposed to – but it gives you an idea of just how difficult it is to be absolutely environmentally ethical where superannuation – or any part of the finance sector – is concerned.

It's simply a warning to 'watch out'. It's the reason you need to look at the holdings of the company you're moving your super to and make sure they're aligned with what you're trying to achieve. Shortly after our conversation, Future Super did ditch Marsh & McLennan, so I'll certainly consider moving my super over to them.

Considering risk when choosing your new super provider

Although value alignment is likely your key priority when you're selecting the right ethical super account for you, this is still ultimately about investing your retirement funds and protecting your future self, so it's important to make a decision that meets your ethical expectations as well as improving your financial position. Regardless of the super provider that you choose, there will be risk associated. That's because all super is invested, and therefore wider economic changes will impact the value of your holdings.

We saw this when the coronavirus pandemic preyed on both our health and our hip pockets. As confirmed cases of the virus rose, stocks plummeted, and this had an immediate impact on everyone's superannuation balances. During March 2020, the share market dropped by a third and the amount of money sitting in our super accounts dipped dramatically. This was more apparent for those of us invested in high-growth assets, which are generally exposed to more volatility than conservative options comprised largely of cash. When you think about risk, one of the most important considerations is most likely your age. If you're in your thirties, like I am, you have a few more decades to contribute to your superannuation. While it could take a few years to recover from these unprecedented economic times, we will see the share market rise and fall several times in the coming decades. Superannuation is a long-term investment and if you're young, you have time for your investment to recover.

If you're nearing retirement, risk will be a bigger concern. To understand how much risk you should take on, it's a good idea to talk to a financial adviser, or a trusted friend or family member, to ensure you're invested in the right product for your circumstances.

How to assess returns and performance

According to superannuation industry research firm SuperRatings, the average fund return was between 13.5 per cent and 14 per cent in 2019. All in all, this was considered pretty great. But it's impossible to predict potential future performance based on the previous year alone. It will not surprise you to learn that in 2020 our super portfolios took a hit in line with the share market, but they did bounce back later that year.

The Australian Securities and Investments Commission (ASIC) highlights some things you can do when you're studying the performance of super funds.

- Look at the fund's performance over at least five years. A fund can have a few great years and then a terrible year. That's not necessarily a bad thing – it happens – but you need to look at results prior to the past year.

- Compare like with like. Look at what the fund is investing in. If the fund you're considering is heavily invested in cash, it's hard to draw a reasonable comparison with one that's invested in shares.

- When it comes to comparing ethical companies, you still need to consider these things before you choose a fund that's aligned with your values. So, make sure you settle on one that's going to look after your nest egg, while also putting that money into businesses that make a difference. It can be easy to get caught up in the ethical impact of the super fund you choose, but it's essential to give equal consideration to your future returns.

The extremely un-sexy subject of fees

Many financial commentators will tell you to simply pick a super fund with low fees. But it's not quite that simple. There are so many things that will impact your fees. This can include basic administration, investment and transaction costs, and a fee for switching providers. Then there are also costs associated with personal advice that your provider can offer, and insurance that you might choose to add to your account. For example, your provider might include total and permanent disability or life insurance products that you can pay for using your super. Of course, you'll want to think about returns as much as you think about fees. If ethical investments continue to outperform the industry benchmarks, you'll want to keep an eye on performance too.

As there are so many variables, it can be tricky to get your head around it, but there are online superannuation calculators to help you understand your current position and how fees and returns might impact you.

Hypothetically, if you have a fee of 1 per cent and a return of 7 per cent, that's okay, but if you pay a fee of 2 per cent and a return of 11 per cent, the higher fee is generally offset by the higher return. There are heaps of variables, but my point is that fees aren't your only consideration – you need to consider fees in the context of returns.

But how do ethical returns offset fees?
Well, the short answer is many ethical funds don't have the historical records that more established super funds do, but even if they did, it wouldn't guarantee anything. So, for example, a huge super fund might have twenty years of historical return data. But a newer ethical fund

might have five years – or less – of return information available. But regardless of how much data they have, the rule of thumb is: past performance doesn't ensure future results. That said, we're seeing early indications that funds investing responsibly are outperforming those that don't. According to the RIAA's 2019 *Responsible Investment Super Study*, thirty-four responsible investment super funds returned an average of 8.14 per cent in a five-year period, while twenty funds that weren't considered responsible returned 7.70 per cent in the same time.

While no scenario is a sure thing, we can see that a higher return from an ethical fund could offset the fees. Either way, performance is in the spotlight. In 2021, the Morrison government introduced its Your Future, Your Super reforms, which are designed to highlight underperforming funds. Looking at performance is critical and it can have a huge impact on your retirement.

You need to do your own research because we can't predict future performance, but if responsible funds continue to outperform other funds, it's important to consider the impact of both fees and returns, not just one or the other.

Gunning for change

Christina Hobbs, co-founder and CEO of Verve Super, has achieved more in the past fifteen years than most people do in a lifetime. After starting her career at Deloitte as a management consultant in 2006, Christina quickly felt a sense that she wasn't doing anything particularly meaningful. She wanted to do more with her skills, so in 2008 she moved to Kathmandu to work as an economist.

'People used to give blankets and food, but the humanitarian response had shifted toward giving people cash to stimulate local economies and buy what they needed,' Christina explains. During this time there was a need to set up sophisticated banking strategies.

'How do we transfer money to those people? How do we make sure money doesn't get into the wrong hands?' she wondered, while working to find solutions.

The idea of good people's money ending up in the wrong hands would continue to be the driving theme of her career, a career that would take many surreal and dangerous turns, particularly during her time working with the United Nations.

'I worked in Somalia during the famine, then on the Syria response based in Turkey. I worked in refugee camps,' she recalls. All extremely noble stuff, but Christina was still frustrated, because she was 'treating the symptoms, not the causes'.

Christina returned to Australia in 2014. She hit the pause button and took a year off to assess her options. 'I started climate campaigning,' she says. At that time, divestment campaigning was really starting to take off too. It began, as all good movements do, with a handful of US college kids making some noise about fossil fuels on campus lawns around 2010. An international movement kicked off, and the Go Fossil Free divestment campaign was born in 2012, with the aim of challenging the fossil fuel industry and encouraging all people to move their money out of 'dirty energy' and into productive solutions.

Since it started, businesses, local governments and individuals have pledged to divest more than $12 trillion in funds and assets out of fossil fuels and into alternatives, according to gofossilfree.org. But Australian superannuation funds were doing absolutely nothing, and every single one, with the exception of Future Super, had investments in fossil fuels.

Christina took the opportunity to join the board at Future Super. 'I started doing some investigations,' she says, explaining that she needed to enhance her knowledge of superannuation investments. By 2015, she had a clear understanding of the overwhelming problems with the existing system.

She returned to Turkey and then Iraq in 2016. 'I was in Baghdad sitting in my shipping container bedroom in the military compound I was living in, listening to choppers and fighter jets all day and night. I decided to come back and start Verve,' she says. 'I was convinced that we needed a global movement of people thinking about capital consciously if we are to rapidly transition our economy and our society to a sustainable, peaceful future.'

Her super, and that of many other Australians, was not only invested in fossil fuels, it was also invested in large-scale weapons companies. 'I'd been on the frontline. I'd been in a refugee camp that got shelled. Knowing my money was invested in weapons was horrifying.'

'Many Australians have their super invested in assault rifles,' Christina goes on. She's talking about the same kind of assault rifle used in New Zealand's Christchurch massacre. 'These companies are well known for lobbying the US government to keep relaxed gun laws,' she adds.

Returning to Australia, Christina began to explore ways to set up her own superannuation fund in January 2018. Something that would have a dual purpose: it would be ethical, but she would also seek to close the superannuation gap between women and men.

While Christina had plenty of the knowledge required, it wasn't something she could do alone, so she called in reinforcements. 'It's not an easy process to start a super fund – which is a good thing because you're investing people's life savings,' she points out.

Christina's first call was to Zoe Lamont, one of Australia's pioneering women-focused financial advisers. Back in 2008, Zoe started 10,000 Girls, a program in which she aimed to educate – you guessed it – 10,000 girls on business and management to foster economic growth. She coached women across the country, in cities and regional towns, and was successful in hitting her target.

Christina had been watching from afar, tracked down her details and called Zoe. 'She was in her rose garden doing some weeding. I told her about the idea and she was in, even though we'd never met,' Christina recalls. Today, Zoe is Verve's co-founder.

With a few more key players invited into the fold, they then engaged a trustee, who holds the money and takes the legal responsibility. To set up the investment arm, they surveyed about 1000 women across Australia to work out what people thought was ethical and to establish what the screening process would be in order to help them to decide what investments were in and what didn't make the cut. By December 2018 they were ready to launch.

You've gotta pay for good service

Ethical super funds are still businesses, so they need you to pay a small sum regularly to cover administration, wages and the work they do for you. Generally speaking, you'll find that ethical funds do charge higher fees than some retail and industry options. There's a couple of reasons for this. Firstly, newly established ethical funds are likely to have fewer members than larger funds. The big guys have more members, and therefore more money invested, which potentially means they can offer lower investment fees.

Secondly, ethical funds also do comprehensive research into where your money is invested. The consistent active screening does take time, and time is money. This is by no means a justification for higher fees, but the time spent assessing your investments may well be something that you see value in.

There are other reasons that fees collected by other super funds that aren't necessarily deemed ethical might be low. For example, some funds invest more in cash than in shares, and the fees are lower because it's cheaper to do this. That could be really important to you if you have a small account balance, but I personally like to consider both returns and fees in my decision-making.

To understand returns, Christina says, you need to think about risk. 'If you look at the market over the past fifty to 100 years, what you see is the more risk you have (i.e. more growth assets and shares than cash), you'd likely have higher returns, but you have higher intermittent risk.'

She believes we're on the edge of a massive shift: that marketing based on low fees is no longer going to cut it. 'A large portion is pure laziness. So many funds have been able to offer low fees because they invest in the top 200 companies and index funds – it's the cheapest way. The notion that it will continue in the face of climate change as it has is really naive. When people are pushing an "invest the cheapest way" message, they're not telling people they're investing in industries that really can't thrive,' she concludes.

Ethical holdings

In just a few clicks I have access to Verve's complete list of holdings. It's divided into categories including renewable energy and energy efficiency, public transport, animal care, education and learning centres, healthcare, food, nutrition and markets, clothing and apparel, banks, insurance and financial services, property and media, information and entertainment.

There's a compelling list of companies on the list. Businesses that I'd be delighted to help bankroll. To name a few: Tesla (electric cars), ZEN Energy (solar power), Cochlear (implantable hearing devices), Netflix (innovative media) and Japara Healthcare (high-quality aged care).

Of course, it's not perfect. There's a few banks in there, although not the big nasty ones. Bank of Queensland is included, and it has lent tens of millions to businesses invested in coalmining, oil and petroleum exploration. In August 2019, it had $31 million invested in companies involved in fossil fuel. However, it has committed to end these loan agreements by the end of 2023.

Then there are property developers, who are not often known for their ethics, but at least those on this list, such as Mirvac and Stockland, have dedicated sustainability programs. Mirvac in particular is making great strides in the sustainable housing space, working on a 'net zero' community in the Melbourne suburb of Altona North. With the help of the Australian Renewable Energy Agency (ARENA), Mirvac will work to build an estate called The Fabric. In phase one, forty-eight townhouses will be built, and once completed they will highlight Mirvac's capacity for constructing net-zero energy houses. If it performs, it could set new benchmarks for residential developers. That's not to say that big developments are necessarily the most ethical of property options, but development will continue to occur because people need housing. If it's energy-efficient, that's some progress.

But when I'm doing my research, I find that Verve is also invested in Marsh & McLennan, the company that planned to insure Adani. I enquire about this, and, like Future Super, they tell me they've recently divested. Good.

I'm not stupid – I know that anyone can whack a sustainability message on their website while simultaneously operating a business that generates millions of tonnes of carbon each year – not every holding is hardcore sustainable – but overall the list of companies that Verve has invested in are impressive, exciting even.

So why do I still feel an element of guilt? Like, should I be giving more to charity instead of focusing on my own wealth? Christina suggests focusing less on the moral angst that comes with a desire to 'get rich' and look more at wealth as a means to 'have an abundance of what you value in your life'. That makes sense. Money provides freedom – the ability to make good choices, to influence others and to hold them to account.

There are many ethical super funds available now, all with varying 'green' portfolios. I like Verve not only for its ethical stance, but for the fact that it supports women. According to the annual Oxfam International report released in January 2020, the twenty-two richest men in the world have more wealth than all the women in Africa.

Verve invests in a World Vision–backed program called the VisionFund. It uses members' superannuation to invest in small businesses that are mostly run by women living in low-income countries. World Vision provides funds to people who might need something as simple as a cow at a much lower interest rate than other lenders. 'Accessing investment capital can be almost impossible for women living on low incomes in low income countries and they can routinely have to pay upwards of 80 or 90 per cent interest, so they're trapped in a cycle,' Christina says. Through the VisionFund, World Vision provides reasonably priced small business loans and business support so they can grow their businesses as well as improving the living conditions for their children. 'Our members' money is utilised to provide the loans and we get the interest returned. Given that the loans are almost always repaid, they have been able to provide a solid return at a relatively low level of risk,' she says.

Do your due diligence

Before you select a super fund that you think is right for your ethical position and financial needs, it's important to drill down into the full picture of the offering. That means reading the product disclosure statement (PDS) and understanding the fees and charges.

In the case of Verve, I understand there is an administration fee of $1.80 per week and an administration and investment fee of 1.19 per cent per annum. It's worth noting, though, that Verve has only one investment option: the Verve Super Balanced Strategy. However, at the time of writing, Verve had submitted two additional products to its trustee for approval.

In the past, some media commentators compared this to Future Super's Balanced Index, which also cost $1.80 per week but charged a lower investment fee of 0.97 per cent per annum, and therefore concluded that Verve charges a 'pink tax' for its female members. But it's not a like-for-like comparison. Future Super's Balanced Index is for fee-conscious members, and while it is a fossil-fuel-free portfolio, it's not as active in terms of really positive ethical investment. One article also compared Verve's fees to the lower fees applied to Hesta's eco portfolio, but Hesta doesn't make its complete portfolio public. According to Market Forces, an independent climate activist group, Hesta only discloses its top twenty Australian and top twenty international shareholdings, so drawing ethical comparisons is impossible.

A fairer comparison would have been between Verve's Super Balanced Strategy and Future Super's Renewables Plus Growth option, which is fossil-fuel-free and also actively invests in renewable projects. When, in 2020, I compare these, Verve comes out on top from a fee perspective, with Future Super charging $1.80 per week plus 1.74 per cent in administration per annum, compared to Verve's $1.80 and 1.21 per cent per annum.

By June 2021, Verve had reduced its fees further, to $1.15 per week and an administration fee of 0.775 per cent per annum, while Future Super was charging $1.15 per week and an administration fee of 1.501 per cent per annum on both its Balanced Impact and Renewables Plus Growth portfolios. Even its low-cost option was higher than Verve's, with its Balanced Index costing $1.15 per week and 0.885 per cent in administration per annum.

I speak to a couple of old-school financial advisers, who point out that Verve's fees (at the time) are higher than some industry funds and urge me to be cautious. And I'm like, 'Alright, I understand that, but why are you all so focused on fees?' None of them seemed hugely interested in the contents of ethical portfolios. It seemed like really short-sighted, shitty advice, but what do I know? My head is spinning from all of this fee chat.

I want to hear what Verve has to say about this, so I speak to Alex Andrews, co-founder and chief operating officer of Verve. 'Fees don't make any sense without the context of returns. If you are charging $20 and you're returning $150, or charging $10 and returning $80, who's better off?' she asks. And although performance in any particular moment doesn't reflect what might happen in the future, I certainly take her point.

'Verve is competitive on fees and returns,' she stresses. 'In 2020, Verve's Super Balanced Strategy had the twelfth-best return out of 214 balanced investment options. This comparison is not just among other ethical options, it's across a range of mainstream funds.' This achievement supports the findings of the Responsible Investment Association of Australia, that ethical funds tend to outperform mainstream funds over all time periods.

However, Alex is also realistic about what it means to be a challenger in an industry of laggards. 'No one is perfect, not even Verve! What we do is centre our members and consider how we can put more money in the hands of women and use our super to invest in the world we want,' she says. That means both building capital to invest in impactful pursuits, like renewables, but also building a community that helps build wealth through education.

Alex adds that businesses that are trying to blaze a trail are also typically focused on innovation and ingenuity, so you get to buy into that too. She tells me that Future Super was the first fund to have an online joining form – and that was as late as 2013, despite the *Electronic*

Transactions Act passing in 1999 and coming into effect in 2000. The big low-cost funds could have whipped up an online form in those seven years, but they didn't.

Look, Alex is right. No super fund is perfect. But I'm not looking for perfection, I'm looking for a fund that wants to do the right thing. A fund that I can hold to account. A fund that is transparent about where my money is invested. I suspect that, over time, ethical funds will become more competitive as more people recognise the value in engaging with the way their super is invested, but they can't do this if people aren't prepared to make the move.

Drawing comparisons between funds can be a flawed exercise, especially when it comes to ethical funds. You really need to do an extensive amount of research into the portfolio, the fees and the history of returns, then ultimately decide what's right for you. It may even be wise to speak to a finance professional, as the PDS documents, fees and portfolios can be overwhelmingly difficult to digest.

Timing your move

It's so damn easy to switch super funds, but does it matter when you do it? Well, as we know, the market goes up and down, so if you're switching like-for-like, the impact should be negligible. The balance of your account on any given day gives you an indication of how your super is performing at that moment (unless of course you are over sixty-five and plan to withdraw the entire balance on the day). Although I'm moving from my existing fund to an ethical fund, they're pretty similar in the respect that I'm transferring from a reasonably balanced portfolio invested largely in shares to another of the same type.

However, had I been moving from the one I'm currently invested in to another fund composed largely of cash, the implications would have been different. If you're concerned about the market at the time you're moving, it might be worth talking to a professional to ensure you nail your timing.

Making the switch

In the end, I move my super over to Verve, and it's incredibly easy. Ultimately, I choose Verve because its holdings are generally aligned with my values, and I'm also impressed with their commitment to the empowerment of women. However, as a reasonably new ethical investment fund, they don't have a long period of historical performance data. When looking at your ethical options, you'll need to consider this, as many ethical funds are only beginning to take off. I decide it's a risk I'm willing to take.

I supply my name, age, address and tax file number, and Verve can access my existing fund, close the account and move my money across. I submit my application and instantly I'm presented with a form highlighting my current super investments; I transfer my entire balance and, just like that, I've invested my super in a fund that I'm happy with.

I'm self-employed, but if I wasn't I'd need to forward details of the change to my employer so they can add payments to my new account. In my case, I will now top it up myself.

The moment it's done, I feel empowered. I wish I could have told my teenage self how important this is. Nonetheless, I'm now on an ethical path and will proactively watch what's happening to my superannuation. That means keeping an eye on what's invested in my portfolio, and looking at fees and performance.

Just because I've moved to Verve doesn't mean I'll stay for good. I now plan to be far more active in monitoring my super, how it's invested and the way in which the additional fees and charges impact my investment. My circumstances may change in time, and I might consider more aggressive options in future. There are no exit fees if I choose to move again. But bouncing around isn't ideal either. For now, I decide to wait and watch. The key is to remain consistently engaged.

Ethical admin checklist

 Read the product disclosure statement. This should be available on each provider's website. Here you'll find all the information about risks, benefits, fees and charges.

 Consider the returns. While past performance is not indicative of future results, seeing how a fund has performed over time is valuable information.

 Make the switch. Once you have made a decision, you can visit your new provider's website and fill in a form to move your super. Once that's done, they generally take care of the rest.

 Stay engaged. Keep an eye on how your super is performing: read the emails they send when they update you on the portfolio. Remember, you don't have to stick with the same super fund if it's not meeting your expectations.

4

Banking on
Bad Behaviour

AS YOU'VE SEEN, MOVING YOUR super from one fund to another is relatively easy. Now it's time to think about who you're banking with.

I've been an ANZ customer since I was a child. Like many Australians, I ended up with the provider that my parents banked with. All of their finances were with the one institution. They'd moved from NAB to ANZ when they'd applied for a home loan. Dad tells me that back then they only had the Big Four (ANZ, CBA, NAB, Westpac) to choose from, although in the late 1980s and early '90s there was a lot more face-to-face interaction, which meant they built a human relationship.

Dad recalls 'Bob the bank manager', who took a great deal of interest in our family's finances. When it came time to open an account for me and my brothers, Bob sorted us out. To be honest, I've always had reasonably positive interactions with ANZ. They helped me through my home loan application, and the people I've dealt with have been really accommodating.

But, of course, the 2018 Royal Commission into Misconduct in the Banking, Superannuation and Financial Services Industry opened my eyes to just how unethical banks can be. Scratching the surface, findings include sales-driven cultures that focused on profit over customers' best interests, poor financial planning advice, ignoring anti-money-laundering and counter-terror-financing laws, foreign exchange trading scandals, failure to pass on benefits and discounts offered in home loan packages, and fraudulent lending to the elderly.

Real classy, banks.

Despite everything, they're still taking the piss. Interest rates are at record lows, but some banks have resisted passing on the cuts in full. Even if they announce that they will, you might still need to ask them to apply that cut to your home loan. Like, seriously, do they want to keep their customers or not?

The big financial institutions have been forced to clean up their act, but inevitably the damage has been done and now consumers are far more aware of what those holding their hard-earned funds are capable of. It's also created an opportunity for small disruptive banks to take advantage of the overwhelming discontent and build new customer bases, by offering ethical alternatives.

There is no question that Australia is lagging behind. In 2019, Larry Fink, chairman and CEO of BlackRock, a global investment management firm, wrote an open letter to investors, highlighting a fundamental need to make changes to investment structures.

Here's a bit of what he had to say:

What will happen to the 30-year mortgage – a key building block of finance – if lenders can't estimate the impact of climate risk over such a long timeline, and if there is no viable market for flood or fire insurance in impacted areas? What happens to inflation, and in turn interest rates, if the cost of food climbs from drought and flooding? How can we model economic growth if emerging markets see their productivity decline due to extreme heat and other climate impacts?

While this is a noble effort, it does not change the painfully slow approach many large-scale organisations are taking to reviewing their investment strategies in light of an uncertain future. Although awareness is growing, a small portion of the population moving their money elsewhere doesn't exactly put a dent in the Big Four's profits. And those profits are contributing to investments that you might not agree with.

Put simply, when you're not spending your money, it's not just quietly sitting there waiting to be withdrawn. Banks take your money and reinvest it in potentially profitable ventures. You have absolutely no say in how this cash is used. In recent years, their investment in fossil fuels has come under serious scrutiny. Since 2008, the Big Four have invested $70 billion in fossil fuel projects, and many people are divesting from their existing bank if it's invested in fossil fuel and moving over to one that's more ethical.

What is divestment?

Divestment is like anti-investing. It's where companies, investors and people consciously pull their money out of stocks or funds whose purpose they don't believe in. There have been massive global campaigns to pull out of fossil fuels in recent years and the cries are getting louder.

According to the goals outlined in the Paris Agreement, the world needs to reduce carbon dioxide emissions by nearly half in the next decade and achieve net-zero emissions by 2050. In late 2019, CEOs and leaders of thirty big banks around the world met and agreed to support the Principles for Responsible Banking, which is in line with the Paris Agreement. That includes the likes of the Commonwealth Bank of Australia (CommBank), which is our biggest financial institution invested in this sector. They're divesting and plan to be out by 2030.

In the meantime, though, the ones that don't shift their models in time might remain invested in fossil fuel ventures that are on the downward slide or collapse all together. They need to decrease their exposure in order to reduce risk.

The complex issue of divestment

Forget your stance on ethics for a moment and think purely about the impact of investment on the economy. In a September 2019 *Financial Times* article, Morgan Stanley's CEO, James Gorman, was quoted as saying, 'If we don't have a planet, we're not going to have a very good financial system.'

But it's not that simple. It's a bit of a chicken and egg situation. We need vast amounts of money to fund a strategic shift to businesses that move us away from systemic ways of life. This includes a realistic transition from fossil fuels to long-term renewable solutions. As much as I want you to move your investments into ethical programs, if we all do it at once, this could have huge economic repercussions.

According to the article, 'An industry-led task force set up by the international Financial Stability Board is coaxing financial institutions and other companies to publish information on the risks climate change poses to their bottom lines.' That transparency is vital, but it will also inevitably provide clear indications as to the economic impact of divesting in an industry that has underpinned global economics for decades.

So why don't the banks just get out now? Financially it makes good sense. The 2018 Global Commission on the Economy and Climate reported that a unified and swift approach to renewable investment could generate $26 trillion in economic gains from now to 2030.

Problem is, we lack a practical and holistic approach. I imagine there's likely a bunch of dinosaur businesspeople sitting in long, boring board meetings trying to work out how to move their investments from coal and oil over to renewables, then ultimately concluding: *It's too hard, let's just stick with the status quo.*

'Current regulations, incentives and tax mechanisms are a major barrier to implementing a low-carbon and more circular economy,' the report points out.

In short, we can't expect our archaic financial institutions to make changes if our governing bodies don't do their jobs and lead. The report recommends that all governments develop clear strategies to transition to improved energy systems.

According to the Liberal Party's website, 'The recent budget [2020/21] invests $1.4 billion for the Australian Renewable Energy Agency to invest in next generation technologies to cut emissions in agriculture, manufacturing, industry and transport.'

Sounds pretty good, but a cruise around Australia's Renewable Energy Target website, where there's a more detailed look at the federal government policy, suggests at least 33,000 gigawatt hours (GWh) of Australia's power would be generated by renewable sources in 2020.

But, to put that in context, according to the Australian government's Department of Environment and Energy, 'Total electricity generation in Australia was estimated to be 261,405 gigawatt hours (GWh) in calendar year 2018.'

So it's safe to say we have a long way to go.

And this inevitably means that for now, at least, we still need fossil fuels if we want to watch Netflix and continue to enjoy the benefits of powering our homes. That's not to say you should be investing in fossil fuels, but they're a necessary evil right now.

Plus, if there was a dramatic shift away from them, it would have a significant short-term impact on the share market and the broader economy. According to a 2015 *Guardian* article by Larry Elliott, 'In the unlikely event that investors all pulled out of fossil fuels at once, the result would be much worse than what followed the collapse of Lehman Brothers in September 2008 – a colossal stock market crash, followed by an equally epic slump.'

He also points out that we, the population, continue to play our part in the problem, even if we divest en masse through our superannuation and investments. Your mobile phone, laptop, television and car all exist thanks to fossil fuels. Whether we like it or not, our lifestyle demands that we keep the fossil fuel sector – and the economy – humming along.

Unfortunately, divestment in things that are unethical doesn't necessarily work unless the same money that would have been invested goes into the ethical alternative.

Fight the power

There are activist groups working to expose the nature of these investments. Take Market Forces, which argues that banks, superannuation funds and governments with the ability to use our money to invest elsewhere should do so to improve our prospects, rather than damaging the environment. Pretty reasonable, really.

The content on the Market Forces website is damning. It provides a comprehensive list of banks, insurance companies and superannuation providers investing in fossil fuels. There's also a section focused on current fossil fuel projects, such as the Adani coalmine, and the companies involved in bankrolling it. They've also created some handy pre-filled forms that allow people to put banks on notice, explaining that they're not happy with their current activities.

Julien Vincent founded Market Forces in 2013 after working at Greenpeace. He worked with the environmental group Friends of the

Earth to get the concept off the ground. Julien was ahead of his time in those early days, but in recent years awareness of consumer funds invested in fossil fuels has well and truly hit the mainstream, with people sharing Market Forces data across social media platforms. Public support is certainly helping Julien and his team get the job done.

We meet in a Melbourne cafe, not far from his head office. I wasn't sure what to expect when preparing to meet an incredibly driven activist, but I find him to be warm and gentle in his approach to sharing his message. He calls bullshit on companies that claim remaining in fossil fuels allows them to influence and drive change. 'The institutional investors have let everybody down. By 2030 our super sector should own half of the ASX and they're doing bugger-all to influence the companies,' he says.

Having said that, he's realistic about the process of banks divesting from fossil fuels but says there should be a strategy in place. 'In five years we need to see companies that have decided they're planning for their demise and starting to experience that demise,' he says.

His company's work is based on years of research. The team packages up that information and shares it in a way that's digestible. Julien says that although there are significant challenges posed by global warming, they're manageable. 'We can work out how we meet a target of 1.5 degrees Celsius and work back from there. Technically, we've got solutions.'

But he also acknowledges that the changes required are more complex than simply divesting, explaining that we need 'societal change in terms of workforce'. That means providing education and skills to those who've perhaps worked in coalmining, and offering practical support so that they're able to transition into roles in renewable energy.

Julien discusses Whitehaven Coal, which brands itself as 'the leading Australian producer of premium-quality coal'. Indeed, it's the biggest listed coalmining company in the country, and most super funds and banks have shares in it. In recent years, the company bulldozed hundreds of hectares of critically endangered forest in north-eastern New South Wales for its Maules Creek coalmine.

Plus, according to Market Forces, in the last four years of available data, Whitehaven Coal has barely paid a cent in corporate tax, even though it's generated more than $6 billion in revenue in that time.

Julien points out that it's widely accepted that if we're going to keep global warming below 1.5 degrees Celsius, we have to phase out coal power globally by 2050. In the medium term, coal production should fall 67 per cent by 2030. Despite this, Whitehaven Coal has more than doubled its output in a bit over half a decade and is planning to expand further through its proposed Vickery project.

The unfortunate reality is there's still money to be made. That's how Whitehaven justifies it, anyway. Besides, as long as they receive the investment required, they have the green light to carry on.

'It should be planning to wind up and they're being encouraged by their investors on our behalf not to do it,' he says.

Am I inadvertently funding this via my banking choices? Yes. And you probably are too. If you, like me, have funds stashed with one of the Big Four banks, you've been enabling this. Like I said, though, I accept that complete divestment can't happen overnight because the economic impacts would be massive. Hilariously, in 2013, environmental activist Jonathan Moylan whipped up a sophisticated hoax ANZ media release claiming the bank had reversed a decision to cough up a $1.2 billion loan for Whitehaven, then he emailed it to journalists.

The result? Whitehaven's share price fell 8.8 per cent and its trading was halted. It bounced back once the fake news was identified, but it gives you an idea of what can happen when divestment isn't managed properly.

Whitehaven's case for continuing isn't nearly as strong as it once was. In December 2019, the company issued a statement that said a skills shortage coupled with challenging weather conditions would impact returns in the 2019/20 financial year. 'Drought continues to place significant pressure on many businesses right across New South Wales, and Whitehaven is not immune to its impacts,' the statement said. According to *The Australian Financial Review*, that announcement wiped $340 million of the company's market value.

Ah, the irony. Climate change is impacting Whitehaven's bottom line. Poor loves.

Back at the bank, the suits were in discussions. It is perhaps no accident that the very next day, documents were leaked. An ABC article by Michael Slezak indicated that ANZ planned to shake off $700 million in coal loans by 2024. I like to think there's a bunch of passionate people on the inside forcing this change and speeding it up via this leak.

There's little doubt that public sentiment is having some influence. Julien says he's seen an incredible turnaround in people's general interest in and awareness of how their money is being used, particularly from 2016 to 2019. He says that he's consistently receiving emails from people saying, 'Thanks for the comparison table, I just moved my money.'

He respects the alternative move, which involves being vocal about your bank's present activities and expressing that in writing. Either approach gives every consumer a level of 'activism and agency'.

'It's empowering to know you can deliver change without having to know who's in the Lodge,' he adds, highlighting that any action you take with your money as an individual really can have an impact. In the same way, one vote might feel tiny on its own but they all add up.

So, in essence, if you're not happy with the way your bank is operating, you can move your money or you can make some noise and try to influence change. Let's look at the pros and cons of each path.

Option A: Move your money

If you're jack of your bank's behaviour and you just want your savings tucked away with a good one, there are some options. But, as always, you'll need to do your own research and look at more than just how they're investing. Maybe you also care about their customer service, how they treat their staff or what their public stance is on a range of issues beyond fossil fuels.

For example, as poor as ANZ's performance has been on fossil fuels, they were one of the largest banks to support marriage equality, alongside the Commonwealth Bank. While this certainly doesn't undo either bank's approach to climate change, the point is you might choose a bank for reasons other than their stance on coal investment.

It's also reasonable to want superior customer service and a seamless tech experience too. Also, fees and charges are a perfectly acceptable consideration. In an ideal world, ethical choices shouldn't make you any worse off.

I'm not here to force an ethical position on you. However, for the sake of simplicity, I'm going to use climate change and fossil fuel funding as the key decision-making factor in the below examples.

There are some great options out there, including Adelaide Bank and Bendigo Bank. But just because they don't invest in fossil fuels doesn't mean they're investing in renewables. It also doesn't mean they're not investing in other questionable ventures. It's a jungle out there, which is why I choose to look at the Market Forces website to explore their comparison table, which allows me to see the position of more than 120 banks, credit unions and building societies.

According to Bank Australia's corporate affairs manager, Cheyne McKee, 'It's been really interesting with the fire situation. People are starting to make that direct connection.' By this Cheyne means that people are increasingly associating massive environmental events, such as the 2019/20 bushfires, with the impact of climate change.

Bank Australia is an example of a bank that's openly saying no to fossil fuels, and it says it's seen the number of new customers increase consistently in the past few years. In some cases, Cheyne says, people talk about it, although he admits there's the final hurdle of actually doing the life admin, but now 'we're seeing the impetus of people to make the change'.

There's a new breed of banks playing in this space, although Bank Australia has been around for more than sixty years, growing out of the credit union movement. At first it was the CSIRO employment credit union. 'A group of scientists got together to work out how they could help each other when the bigger banks were strict with their lending,' Cheyne explains. Since then seventy-two credit unions have joined.

In 2011, Bank Australia officially became the first customer-owned bank in the country, which means customers have a say in how the business is run. 'When it comes time to vote for directors, every customer has their vote,' Cheyne says. In the aftermath of the banking royal commission, it's certainly become an attractive option for consumers. Rather than operating with a profit motive, they're operating with a customer motive.

At a fundamental level, Bank Australia operates like any other bank. They take the money people deposit and pay them interest, loaning it out for other purposes. The difference is where that money goes. 'Our customers can be confident that if they don't want to see fossil fuels expand, their money is never going to be put to that use,' Cheyne says. Instead, they invest in sustainable and affordable housing, the disability and social housing sectors and renewable energy. However, he admits, 'Our scale is comparatively small.' Bank Australia is often looking at projects on a community level – small solar and wind projects, for example. It sources the renewable energy that powers its business through the Melbourne Renewable Energy Project – a windfarm in Victoria called Pacific Hydro – a project that NAB and the Commonwealth Bank were part of too.

While the result of the project enabled Bank Australia to become the first Australian bank running on 100 per cent renewable energy, the majority of the funding came from NAB and CommBank.

This is the challenge. The Big Four banks are much better placed to invest in ethical ventures on a massive scale than the smaller ones – the problem is that they're not doing nearly as much as they could. So the question is: do I want to stay with my big bank in the hope they sort their shit out and divest from fossil fuels and start pumping cash into renewables, or do I move to a smaller outfit that's at least committed to doing good work, even if it's on a small scale?

According to Australian Ethical, a leading ethical super fund, there are justifications for continuing to invest in larger banks – some of them, at least. Australian Ethical assesses all of its investments against its ethical charter, which hasn't changed since the company was founded in 1986. The charter highlights twelve things the company supports, and eleven things it avoids based on the fact that these things are harmful.

They argue, 'Investment in clean energy totalled more than $19 billion for large scale renewable projects underway in Australia in 2019, equating to 13,725 jobs across the country.'

Australian Ethical says that Westpac, for all its flaws, has still been the largest financier of greenfield renewable energy projects in Australia in recent years. They've committed $9.3 billion to solutions that will change our approach to climate change and they have an ambitious goal of spending $25 billion by 2030. That's a solid effort when you compare it to the investment plans floated by other banks. In 2019, more than 75 per cent of Westpac's electricity sector lending was going to renewable projects.

According to Amanda Richman, ethics analyst at Australian Ethical, in order to limit global warming to a rise of 2 degrees Celsius, as part of the Paris Agreement, more than US$1 trillion needs to be invested in clean energy every year through to 2050. 'Smaller Australian banks simply aren't able to fund large-scale clean energy infrastructure. They just don't have the capacity to make loans for big projects – whether climate friendly or not,' she says.

'We will only invest in banks which we assess to be aligning their business lending activities with the Paris Agreement. This can be complicated to assess because of the scale and diversity of lending by large banks,' she adds.

At Australian Ethical, they use a 'climate scorecard' to assess lending to the fossil fuel sector, renewable energy and storage, and technologies that reduce energy usage or store carbon, such as 'green' buildings, low-emissions transport and reforestation.

'Specific factors we consider include loans to the mining sector and to coal as a percentage of the total loan book, the ratio of fossil fuel to renewable lending, the ranking of the bank's climate governance (assessed by Boston Common Asset Management), and the way the bank facilitates financing by others, for example by arranging the issue of green bonds,' Amanda explains.

They also look at the banks' public support for government climate change policy in line with the Paris Agreement. She points out that currently the Paris Agreement doesn't mean a bank can't lend to fossil fuel interests. 'The transition pathway is different for different types of fossil fuels,' Amanda says. Take, for example, thermal coal versus gas. In the short term, gas can be used to support renewable energy supply.

'There are of course "no-go projects" that are clearly not aligned. For example, we do not, and will not, invest in any bank which lends to the Adani Carmichael coalmine,' Amanda says.

The Australian Ethical approach to investing in banks is selective, and in investing in them, they also advocate for improvement. 'While we currently assess that Westpac and NAB are lending in line with the Paris Agreement climate goals, we generally support the Market Forces shareholder resolutions that ask the banks to be more open about how they are implementing this commitment,' Amanda points out.

I understand this. I believe it's important to divest from fossil fuels, but if we were somehow magically able to do this all at once, the economic impact would be catastrophic. You only have to look at the sudden plummet of the share market due to Covid-19 to understand this in practice. Having said that, I'm certain that there is not enough being done in Australia to strategically tackle the shift, and I want to know how it can be done as fast as possible with minimal impact on the economy.

'This is why transition pathways to net zero, and science-based targets, are so important. There are many research organisations working on developing transition pathways for different sectors, including the International Energy Agency,' Amanda explains. She suggests a sudden transition would result in workers without jobs, communities without a core industry and 'stranded assets, contributing to rising inequality, economic stagnation and instability'.

But Australia lags behind. Amanda points to Germany, where there has been a strong strategy and timeline for phase-outs. The country has already phased out black-coal mining completely and has a timeline to phase out brown coal. People have been reskilled and deployed elsewhere. The communication has been consistent and effective. Meanwhile, in Australia, 'there is broad recognition (among trade unions, energy companies and green groups) that the demise of coal is inevitable, although they disagree on the timeframes,' Amanda laments.

'The government is finding ways to support the coal regions and to create new jobs and industries. Of course, this is made easier by the fact they have given themselves plenty of time to do it,' she concludes.

So, we're in a real bind here. I think we can agree that the lack of transition policy is unacceptable at this point. While some banks are doing their bit, others know they have the luxury of time. It's possible that people shifting their money out of banks with huge fossil fuel investment could create a sense of urgency.

Should all Australians with bank accounts move their money over to banks that appear to be truly invested in a sustainable future, or is there merit in staying with a bank that sometimes does shitty things but also has the funds to make a real difference?

When it comes to making that call, it again depends on your personal ethics and your financial situation. Prior to 2020, I was mouthing off about the Big Four banks like so many others, but I was forced to bite my tongue as Covid-19 wrapped its infected tentacles around sole traders, small-business owners and those working for companies that were forced to let their staff go. When the Australian Banking Association's CEO, Anna Bligh, announced on 20 March that banks would defer loan repayments for all small businesses for six months, I immediately wondered how the smaller independent banks would fare.

As someone who was worried about my own income and mortgage, I have to admit I was glad to be banking with an organisation that was in a position to stay afloat for as long as required, all while helping people who were battling through an unprecedented economic crisis. I was also glad to be with a bank that enabled me to stop making mortgage repayments when my investment sat empty. I had three months to list my property and sell it without having to deal with the mortgage, while also covering the rent where I lived.

That said, selling also presented me with an opportunity to look at the alternatives. In dissolving my mortgage, only my savings account and emergency credit card would be tied to the bank, thus making it much easier for me to walk away if I found a better alternative at the end of the process.

How to switch

There are lots of smaller banks providing services for those who want to move their money to a bank whose values they feel more aligned with. Cheyne tells me it's pretty easy to open a new transaction account. In most cases you'll just need a couple of forms of ID, such as a driver's licence, passport and Medicare card. Then it's a matter of moving your cash out of the old one and into the other, remembering to flick all of your direct debits over to the new account, provide your updated banking details to your employer and, of course, close the old account.

The refinancing of home loans and credit cards can be a little bit more complex. Essentially, you have to go through a new credit check. This is going to prove difficult for me at this moment in time. I have a home loan and, honestly, I'm not confident that I could successfully refinance with another bank right now because I'm self-employed. So if I'm going to transition to an ethical bank, the full process could take a while.

Chenye says that when you're looking for a new bank, it's a good idea to look beyond their investment in fossil fuels. Does the bank lend responsibly? Do they have sales targets for their staff? Do they pay hefty bonuses?

Option B: Let your bank know you're pissed off

If I wasn't selling my property, I wouldn't be in a position to move my money, even if I wanted to. My income has fluctuated wildly for three years now, and while I always make sure I'm putting money into my savings and paying my bills on time, refinancing a mortgage loan of hundreds of thousands of dollars is absolutely not an option.

Many people are in a similar position. The pandemic put countless people in the most precarious financial position of their lives. I paused my home loan repayments so I could get through the terrifyingly uncertain time, and I was grateful to be banking with an organisation that gave me that option.

I could at least open a savings account with another bank, though. That said, when you have a mortgage you might have an offset account like I do, which is like a savings account, and when spare cash is stashed there, it reduces the interest you pay on your mortgage. This is, I have realised far too late, a very clever way to keep me loyal.

At the very least, this gives me a cautionary tale to pass along to you. If you are considering a home loan, that's potentially a thirty-year commitment to a bank, so make sure you're happy with what they're able to do for you before you sign on the dotted line. That's not to say you can't move during the life of the loan if you're in a good position, but sometimes, if you choose an unconventional path or unforeseen circumstances change everything, your options are diminished.

Until I sold my property, I had no choice but to stay put with my current bank. But I could do my best to antagonise. Also, my personal view is this: my bank has a *lot* of money. It's wielding the power potentially to do far more than the likes of Bank Australia or Bendigo Bank. I want my bank to do the right thing. I want it to use its influence for good. I also want to do my part to campaign for this.

Vinay Shandal, a partner at Boston Consulting Group in Toronto, presented a TED Talk in October 2018 that enforces the power of taking this approach. He highlights the Chicago Teachers' Pension Fund, a $10 billion fund that took a strong stance on private prisons. Among the many issues with US private prisons, children have been taken from their parents at the US border and placed in private detention. In addition, a privately owned institution may prioritise profit over reasonable care and justice. 'They just sold their stock. Selling did nothing.' he says. In fact, Shandal points out, the stock continued to climb.

The worst part, he says, is that conscious investors owned the stock. They had the power to influence. Inevitably the stock gets snapped up by someone else – someone who potentially doesn't care. 'You can't divest your way to a greener world,' Shandal adds, and argues that conscious investors need to go from divesting to engaging if they really want to drive change.

The same goes for banks. If I don't bank with ANZ, someone else will. I can stay and hold them to account. The jury's out on how effective this is, though. Perhaps you want to write a letter, which is a start, but again, it might not get further than the bank's mailroom trash.

Social media is an obvious place to have your thoughts heard. Power to you if you're an influencer with a platform to reach a huge audience – just do it responsibly, please.

And me? Well, I'm in the position to provide all of this information in book form in the hope it provides you with enough knowledge to make an informed decision.

According to an ANZ spokeswoman, 'ANZ's leadership has made it unequivocally clear that the bank's thermal coal exposure has and will continue to significantly reduce over time.' ANZ did release a statement in November 2020 highlighting commitment to reducing carbon emissions, with the aim of halting the rise in global average temperature and keeping it below an increase of 2 degrees Celsius. However, according to Market Forces, ANZ financed 93 per cent more new fossil fuel projects in 2017 than they did in 2016, with a total of $905 million invested.

'This reduction has not been in a straight line as that is not the nature of these businesses, so we have aimed for continued reductions in line with our recent trajectory,' the spokeswoman said.

'Since 2015, ANZ has funded and facilitated $19.1 billion in environmentally sustainable solutions; including "green" buildings, low emissions transport, green bonds and renewable energy projects.'

To be clear: that's $3.82 billion a year. Not enough when compared to the $9.3 billion Westpac committed in two years alone.

'ANZ has set a new target to fund and facilitate at least $50 billion in sustainable solutions for customers by 2025. This includes initiatives that help lower carbon emissions, improve water stewardship and minimise waste,' she concludes.

In October 2020, ANZ did make a major policy change, committing to phasing out its exposure to thermal coal by 2030, following the lead of other big banks, but it is yet to set targets to reduce its investment in oil and gas.

No matter which way you slice it, most of the major banks are tangled in a web of declining industries and, in the short term at least, it's hard to see how any can make effective dramatic shifts. As I've said, divestment is complex. If you want to be with a bank that's truly disruptive in the way it invests and profits, you'll likely need to consider some of the new market players.

Ethical admin checklist

 Find out what your bank invests in. Market Forces is among the best sources of this information.

 Choose your approach. If you're not happy with your bank, will you switch or put pressure on your bank to be more accountable? It's up to you.

 Work out if you're in a position to move. Your current financial position may prevent you from making a clean switch if that's the path you want to choose. Refinancing credit cards and mortgages with another bank can be complex. Speak to a financial adviser or mortgage broker if you're unsure.

 Research alternative banks. Like superannuation funds, banks have their nuances, pros and cons. Consider the whole ethical landscape before you move.

5

Digital Banking Disruptors

AS A KID, I REMEMBER GOING into the bank with my parents and drawing on deposit slips with a pen that was chained to the benchtop while they wrote cheques and deposited or withdrew money. It's hard to believe that's how we managed cash just a few decades ago, and it's no surprise that digital disruptors are entering the market, providing nimble alternatives to the Big Four.

These startups, many of which emerged in 2018 and 2019, are known as neobanks. That means they operate almost entirely within smartphone apps and mobile pay functions, and have no need for retail branches or traditional physical presences. To take your money, they need to have obtained an authorised deposit-taking institution (ADI) licence from the Australian financial services industry regulator APRA (Australian Prudential Regulation Authority) or work under the licence of another banking institution.

Here's a breakdown of the top three neobanks in Australia:

Volt

Volt Bank was the first neobank to be issued with a restricted ADI licence by APRA after it was founded in 2017. It got a full licence to operate as an authorised deposit-taking institution on 21 January 2019. At this stage, it provides savings account services.

Up

Launched in 2018, Up is the result of a partnership between software company Ferocia, and Bendigo Bank and Adelaide Bank, and offers app-based saving and spending.

86 400

As of 2019, 86 400 became an authorised deposit-taking institution. It was the first Australian neobank to offer home loans and also provides the usual savings account features you'd expect. It's now owned by NAB, which may have an impact on your decision-making if you're looking for ethical banks.

Why neobanks are thriving

With much lower overheads than traditional banks, neobanks can put their time and funding into a seamless digital experience. Many bolted out of the gates with impressive interest rates on savings, driving swift sign-ups around the country. And, of course, millennials and gen Z are so adept at digital banking that they expect the best in digital services and they're moving their money in huge numbers.

How ethical are neobanks?

The ethical issues surrounding neobanks are different to those of the Big Four. They're presently too small to be pouring tonnes of funds into fossil fuels, so you're pretty safe on that front. What they offer is little to no paper wastage and reduced carbon emissions as a result of being 'virtual'. To win your custom they know they need to do things right, so many are positioning themselves – as more than just banks, they're also often framed as companies that can help you gain control of your money and improve your financial wellbeing.

Here are some things to look for in a neobank:

- A competitive interest rate on savings

- Transparency and a strong digital user experience

- Tools and features that enable you to manage your money easily

- Genuine interest in supporting customers to achieve their financial goals

- Strong security features.

Banking for a new generation

I'm about to get a modern banking lesson from a swing-dancing vegan.

I've arrived at a heritage-listed building in South Melbourne to meet Xavier Shay, software engineer at tech company Ferocia, also the home of the neobank Up. Ferocia, an internet banking software company, was founded by two blokes called Dom Pym and Grant 'Thomo' Thomas. Xavier worked for them about ten years ago and he's returned as part of the leadership team that's driving Up's success.*

The moment I meet Xavier he smiles wide. He's tall and lean – no doubt a result of the vegan diet and swing dancing. He's wearing a T-shirt, jeans and sneakers. The look is capped off with a head of

---

* Xavier went on to become CEO of Up and the company is now fully owned by Bendigo Bank.

unruly wavy hair, peppered with just a handful of silver strands.

Xavier begins our tour of the office and I take in the open-plan space, the stairs to the mezzanine and the pressed-metal ceiling. There's a giant couch, and a kitchen where the team tries to eat together at least three times a week. To the back of the building there's a gym where the trainer's working with a staff member. It's eleven a.m.

'It's important for people to take care of themselves,' Xavier says. And if that means a midmorning sweat sesh, then that's cool.

'We're going to move in the next couple of weeks. We love it but we've run out of desks,' he tells me. Ferocia's staff numbers have hovered at around twenty for most of its existence, but when Up launched in 2018, everything changed.

I follow Xavier up a narrow spiral staircase to one of the 'outdoor meeting rooms', which is actually a balcony. It's the perfect spot for a chat. It's a sunny autumn morning and I'm happy to kick back on a couch and hear the Up story.

Ferocia has provided Bendigo Bank's digital banking technology for more than half a decade. 'A couple of years ago, we pitched an idea to them: you provide the financial licence and we'll provide the marketing, project management and customer experience. They agreed. It was a pretty big deal,' Xavier says.

That's an understatement. Most banking bigwigs aren't sticking their necks out for little tech startups. But they had a solid relationship and the founding of Up wasn't a threat to Bendigo, a bank with a customer base largely composed of baby boomers and regional business owners.

'They're not getting the under-thirty-five bracket,' Xavier says. In fact, most banks aren't doing a good job of engaging younger people. Not in a really meaningful way. 'From the start, we said we're going to build this bank in a way we feel like it should be built,' he adds.

Up was one of the first neobanks in Australia. It was set up quickly thanks to its backing from Bendigo Bank and Adelaide Bank, which enabled the business to bypass the wait for a banking licence.

Up became Australia's first cloud-hosted bank. Although the team would operate under Bendigo's licence, there was still much to be done to bring Up to life. For starters, they had to work with Google on a brand-new facility to cloud-host the bank. They also had to work with APRA to ensure Up was in line with the necessary banking standards.

'We introduced Google and APRA,' Xavier says. Up was launched in 2018 and the volume of new customers has been massive. At the time of my chat with Xavier, they have between 500 and 1000 people opening an account via the app every day, and 400,000 active users.

Xavier asks if I've tried it yet and I tell him I'm still considering my options. 'We'll fix that before you leave,' he says confidently, and then reassures me, 'You're just trying out an app.'

His case for giving it a go is pretty convincing: 'The cost to you is three minutes of your time. If you don't like it, you just stop using it. There's no cost to you to open the account.'

On the flip side, he's realistic about what I can do as a customer. Xavier, like me, has a mortgage and Up doesn't provide mortgages, credit cards or business banking. 'I still have another bank too,' he says.

'We want to start by doing one thing really well. That thing should help people: saving and spending,' Xavier says. They've certainly found a gap in the market and played to that. Given the state of the world, the cost of housing and the overwhelming nature of personal finance, it's surprising that larger banks weren't addressing this need sooner. Managing money has become the centre of the cultural zeitgeist for young people trying to get ahead.

In fact, in the past few years we've seen the rise of people known as 'finfluencers' – financial influencers. They're building huge social media communities in which they share what they know about money and investments. Usually they're doing it with really accessible, fun videos and infographics, which make understanding the process of everything from budgeting to buying shares easy to digest. It's worth noting, however, that these people often aren't qualified financial advisers, and therefore they're not giving tailored financial advice. They're not a replacement for traditional advice, but they quite often provide plenty of inspiration.

Like these finfluencers, Up aims to provide financial support in a fun, engaging and supportive way. That includes things like mobile push notifications that provide a bank balance when people spend. They're not the only bank that does this, but they also auto-generate spending behaviour insights, showing people what their cash is going towards.

Up also allows people to create as many savings accounts as they want. Again, this is not an exclusive feature, but I'm drawn to the fact that I can name the account whatever I like and add an emoji. For example, maybe you're saving for a surfboard and you have a goal of $200. Xavier says you can add your target amount and your surfboard emoji. There's also a progress bar indicating how close you are to your target.

The bank's initial aim isn't to get customers to put great wads of cash in their account. They understand their customer base, which is largely made up of students, shiftworkers, part-timers, freelancers and young people in entry level roles. 'That's why we don't have home loans. There's a journey. We don't want our first interaction to be "Do you want a home loan?"' Xavier says. They want to educate their customers, teach them how to manage their money, save for goals, build savings responsibly and incrementally. That's not to say they won't do home loans and larger personal loan offerings in the future. They will grow with their customers as they get older. 'We can help you understand what's reasonable to borrow. At some point the home loan becomes a natural discussion point,' he believes.

From an ethical standpoint, Up is looking at more than avoiding fossil fuel investment. 'You need to be able to trust that we can keep operating as a business,' he says. Initially, that's their priority. The way they make money is interesting. Up doesn't charge a monthly account fee, an ATM withdrawal fee or international transaction fee. Xavier says they can do without these fees currently because they have a small cost base and no branches.

But it's not that simple. Up is backed by Bendigo Bank, and like all banks, they use your deposit to generate loans. They charge interest on those loans and profit from the interest. Because Up has that stable support, they can forgo traditional fees and charges to build their base. It doesn't make them bad; it makes them a business that's striving to be sustainable. The key to that sustainability, Xavier hopes, is the way in which Up engages and empowers customers' money habits by making the process fun.

What I like about Up is their commitment to their customers' financial wellbeing. They want you to save, they want you to do well. That's a completely different mindset to most of the larger banks, which are inevitably prioritising profits. Up meets two aspects of my ethical investment criteria: it's backed by an institution that doesn't invest in fossil fuels, and it's a progressive product that's focused on customers' financial empowerment.

So Xavier invites me to set up my account. He does this through their 'Hook up a mate' referral program. He plugs my phone number into the app and I get a notification. When I accept, we both get $5. If I make a purchase in the next thirty days, Xavier gets another $5.

I follow the link that's been sent to my phone, download the app, choose my 'Up Name' and enter a couple of personal details. I get a notification explaining that my new bank card will be delivered to my home address in the coming days. I set up Apple Pay, then transfer some money from ANZ into my account to distribute into my 'savers'. Up's savers are like mini accounts that you can spread your savings across. You get to name them in line with your goals – bills, house deposit, holiday fund, whatever you're working towards.

I set up a saver called 'Invest for Good'. That's where I'll put savings so that I can build enough to invest in the share market.

Can I trust neobanks?

There are some fairly reliable levels of protection when it comes to neobanks. Any company that positions itself as a banking institution has to be an ADI. These ADIs are approved by APRA. The authorisations aren't just handed out, they're hard-earned and meticulously vetted. In addition, cash held by an ADI is covered in part by the federal government. Through the Financial Claims Scheme, deposits of up to $250,000 per account holder are protected by the government in the event that the bank closes. So your neobank savings are pretty safe.

Digital security is another key consideration. Australian neobank operators know that their security measures are essential to their success in building and maintaining their customer base. Many invest heavily in ensuring their security is completely robust. However, as for any platform you use to manage your money, it's still important that you do your research before making the switch.

You'll also want to think about your personal banking needs. For example, when I'm looking to buy a new home, Up can't help me, so I'm potentially going to have cash in Up, but my mortgage will be elsewhere. I speak to Clara Tang, who's in a similar position. She'd been with one of the Big Four and 'had an itch' to move. 'The only reason I had been with the other bank was for legacy and comfort,' she says.

Clara admits that Up's branding and communications caught her attention. Working in advertising, she loves great design and a seamless user experience. At the time she was researching her options, the savings interest rate and the digital user experience sealed the deal. She also has a mortgage, so Clara arranged for her salary to go into her Up account each month, and she distributes funds into the individual saver accounts she's set up, while also transferring the necessary amount into her mortgage when it's due. 'I see my savings as a buffer – I can take money out to supplement my little luxuries,' Clara says. She has a saver for her pets and one for social spending with her partner. Overall, she doesn't have a huge issue with having more than one financial provider. But it was important to ensure that the neobank was safe. 'I'm dealing with smaller amounts of money in my Up account, but being backed by Bendigo Bank, there's stability that I can trust,' Clara tells me.

Your individual circumstances may dictate which bank you choose and why. For example, if I was able to secure a mortgage with Bank Australia, I'd likely open up a savings account with them too, so that all of my funds were located in one place. For now, I'm working with a mortgage broker to see which bank I might be able to get a loan with, and that may dictate my strategy in the future. For now, I'll put small amounts into my Up savers until my broader financial options are clearer.

Fees and savings interest rates

At the time I open my Up savings account, the 'Up Savers bonus rate' is 1.85 per cent per annum for customers who make five or more purchases per calendar month, and this can be done using the debit card or with digital wallet transactions, such as Apple Pay. It's applied to savings of up to $50,000. For those who don't complete five transactions per month, or have more than $50,000 in their account, the base rate of 0.10 per cent applies.

Up doesn't offer the most competitive interest rates on savings. If you're depositing only small funds, that might not be an issue.

Some financial advisers will say that earning interest on your savings is a really important consideration. If you have hundreds of thousands in the bank, then it's definitely essential to look at the interest rate because you can potentially earn a lot of interest on those savings.

Prior to selling my investment property, I probably wouldn't have thought much about savings interest rates, but when I settled at the time of sale, a large sum was transferred into my account and would remain there until I made my next purchase. For me, Up didn't make the cut in terms of competitive interest rates. That said, with interest rates being so low, most interest rates on cash haven't been great for a while. If I'd been holding a lump sum for longer, like more than year, I might have considered putting it into ethical shares to get a better return. If you happen to be holding strong savings for an extended period, it may be worth looking at where you can invest for better returns. We'll discuss that in the coming chapters.

In the end, I use my Up account to add small amounts of savings purely to see a clear distinction between my play money and the funds I've put aside to invest, but eventually I'll move that money into shares.

On the whole, I think neobanks are great for managing small funds, but as your financial situation becomes more complex, so does your banking behaviour. Nonetheless, in my experience, they're a great alternative to the big guys, especially if you're just starting to improve the way you manage your money, because they offer heaps of great budgeting features, which I like as I begin to allocate my funds effectively across my super, savings and shares.

The future of neobanks

For many neobanks, the increasing competition in the market may present some challenges – and even, in the worst-case scenario, contribute to their demise. Look at the example of Xinja, which announced in late 2020 that it would close, refund bank balances to customers and end its banking licence. According to *The Australian Financial Review*, 'Xinja failed in part because it started taking deposits before it made loans. That meant it had to pay interest to customers before it started generating income.'

It's still difficult to say which neobanks will thrive in the years to come. First, they have to build a market share, then they have to maintain it. Key factors will include strong consumer trust – when it comes to deciding where to put your hard-earned cash, you want to be certain that it'll be protected. Additionally, the established traditional banks are catching on, and have the funds to improve their digital products and services. In many cases, people feel more comfortable staying with a legacy bank because it has the history and the size that neobanks don't.

Ethical admin checklist

 Check the neobank's licence. Any company calling itself a bank must have one, but you'll want to do your own research to be sure.

 Is it ethical? Neobanks don't necessarily operate to the ethical standards that you hold. You'll need to look into whether the bank's operations align with your values.

 Consider the fees and savings interest rate. Many neobanks have offered competitive savings interest rates to lure customers, but these change over time, so keep an eye on any potential creeping costs.

 Does it provide all the products and services you need? The neobank you choose might have a great app or cool features, but if you have a credit card or a mortgage and the neobank doesn't offer these services, you'll need to decide if you're happy to have funds with multiple institutions.

6

Micro-investing

THE 'AUSTRALIAN DREAM' IS SUPPOSEDLY to own a house with a barbecue in your backyard. I had been *obsessed* with this. But it's just so hard to achieve these days. And if it's your only investment and anything goes wrong in terms of market performance or your personal finance situation, you might be back at square one. That was the prospect I faced when I unexpectedly needed to sell my investment at the beginning of the pandemic. Times have changed. We simply cannot rely on property as our entire wealth strategy, especially as it's so hard to penetrate the market in the first place. That doesn't mean the dream is over, it's just changing. I still believe property is a valuable consideration. You need somewhere to live, particularly in your later years, but there are lots of other ways to build wealth, especially if you're starting with limited funds.

Right now, I don't have a large amount of money to put into a comprehensive share portfolio, so I seek out ways to start small while I work towards my bigger savings goal.

If this is totally new to you, a share is basically a unit in a share of a company, fund or asset. When you buy a share, you own a minuscule slither of that company. And because you're a shareholder, you get your share of the profits the company makes – that's how you get a return on your investment. Shareholder profits are known as dividends. In ideal circumstances, you buy your share, the company makes epic profits, you earn dividends and your share goes up in value – so when you sell it, you get more than you paid for it.

In regular circumstances, you probably just want to be buying shares in companies that are expected to perform well. But, as we know, with ethical investments, you need to apply your personal ethics screening process to decide if they're worthy of your commitment.

Before I can decide which shares I'd like to put my money into, I have to be clear on my value set. I call financial adviser Alex Jamieson. He describes the ethical space as a 'spectrum', where it's possible to be 'deep green' at one end and a little more grey at the other. He points out that shares that aren't really green aren't necessarily terrible. They're what he calls 'neutral', meaning they are neither really progressive nor really bad. An example might be Telstra, which is not particularly green or innovative, but is not tearing down rainforests.

Next, he tells me to consider the 'triangle of performance, fees and ethical screen'. Obviously, I want anything I invest in to perform. Fees are also part of the consideration, but as we established earlier, sometimes fees play a part in time spent deep-diving into the quality of the investment. Alex tells me that exchange traded funds (ETF) are a good place to start.

An ETF is a fund that owns assets, which are then divided into shares that you can purchase through the ASX (Australian Securities Exchange), via your brokerage account. The number of units you hold represents your share in the fund. We'll go into more detail about ETFs shortly, but essentially, the reason they're good for a beginner investor is because there's a low barrier to entry and they give you a lot of exposure to different companies.

If you search 'Australian ethical ETFs' online, you'll find heaps of information covering what's available and how they perform. The advantage of choosing ETFs is that it's easy to find specific information about their holdings. A lot of micro-investment platforms have ETF portfolios, and they allow you to buy a tiny share of one using the smallest amount of money.

Let's look at how it works.

What is micro-investing?

Micro-investing enables you to put small amounts of money into an investment portfolio. This is great for people starting out with limited funds, because some traditional share trading platforms require a minimum investment of, say, $500 or $1000 just to get started. But we're talking about investing with tiny sums. Like, you can start with a dollar, or 50 cents. Money that, theoretically, you won't miss. Think spare change that you'd throw into a busker's hat without giving it a second thought.

So with micro-investing you don't have to wait to save up a chunk of cash. Some platforms enable you to 'round up' cents left over in a transaction. For example, you might buy a coffee for $4.50. If you have your transaction account linked to a micro-investing platform, you can set it to round up each purchase to the nearest dollar, so 50 cents goes into your portfolio. The idea is that it's such a small amount, you don't miss it, and the total will grow slowly over time.

It's the perfect way for me to start exploring shares. I'm treating it as my learner driver's licence. It allows me to get into the habit of investing and to build confidence over time, before I hit the investment freeway.

Micro-investing is increasing in popularity, not least because there are some great apps out there that allow you to get started in a matter of minutes. A quick online search reveals a range of options, including Raiz Invest, Spaceship Voyager and Stake. I choose Raiz Invest because, after a bit of reading, I find that they have a dedicated ethical investment portfolio. Plus, there's a handy tool that allows me to round up every purchase that I make and add to my little pot of cash. But before I go any further, there's some basic investment jargon that I need to understand.

Risk assessment

There's always going to be a level of risk when you're investing. The stock market consistently rises and falls. Your risk tolerance will depend on a few factors, including your age, the amount of money you have and the length of time you're prepared to invest it for. In my case, I'm in my thirties, so I have years of work ahead of me and time to make more money. I can also continue to build my portfolio over decades, which means I can take on more risk than someone who's nearing retirement age and can't afford a sudden market drop.

According to ASIC, much of the risk will depend on the period of time you are invested in the market. Here's a quick breakdown of what someone in each investment category should be looking for:

Short-term investor (one to three years)
- Risk: very low risk of losing your money
- Volatility: very low, unlikely the value of your savings will fall
- Expected return: 2 to 3 per cent per year (long-term average return)

Medium-term investor (four to six years)
- Risk: medium possibility of losing some of your money
- Volatility: medium; capital value could go up or down 20 per cent in a year
- Expected return: 4 to 5 per cent per year (on average over ten years)

Long-term investor (seven or more years)

- Risk: high, with negative returns expected four to five years out of twenty
- Volatility: high, capital value could go up or down by 40 per cent in a year
- Expected return: 5 to 6 per cent per year (on average over 10+ years)

Looking at these options, I consider myself a long-term investor, which means I'll hopefully be in a position to weather even the harshest storm. At the time I start looking at the share market, we're deep in the pandemic. You'd think this would be a ridiculous time to consider investing but, actually, market plunges can be beneficial when it comes to buying shares, because they might be more affordable than they'd be in a strong market. Having said that, even if I'd bought shares prior to the pandemic, I would aim to hold them rather than selling. Share prices rise and fall all the time. This is not something to fear. If you're holding your shares for years, history shows that you should end up with a return.

Portfolio

Your portfolio is the bundle of assets that you've invested in. It might include stocks, bonds, cash and other investments. Most portfolios will include a combination of these things so that all of the money you invest isn't in one place: it's a 'diversified' selection of asset classes. When you have a diverse portfolio, it means only a percentage of your overall portfolio could be impacted by market changes at any one time. For example, the value of your shares might drop temporarily, but the cash in your portfolio could remain strong.

Once you've established your level of risk, you're able to decide on the portfolio type. These range in risk from conservative to aggressive. Someone who wants to minimise their risk would likely choose something at the conservative end of the spectrum. I can afford to be slightly more aggressive – not because I have a lot of money, but because I'm in a position to hold onto my portfolio for a long period of time. Let's say I have my portfolio for the next twenty years: the share market will rise and fall a number of times, but in the long run I'm likely to end up with far more than I started with, simply because I've held my investments.

Choosing a micro-investment portfolio

I download Raiz, plug in my bank details and explore my portfolio options. These include conservative, moderately conservative, moderate, moderately aggressive, aggressive and emerald (the socially responsible option).

As above, the conservative portfolio consists largely of cash and corporate bonds, which are exposed to less volatility, while the aggressive portfolio has a big chunk of Australian and Asian stocks, which could be exposed to more significant rises and falls.

Naturally, I choose the emerald portfolio, which is made up of stocks in Australian and global socially responsible investments. To develop the portfolio and ensure the investments are ethical, Raiz uses positive and negative screening to establish which companies make the cut. The emerald portfolio is a combination of two ETFs – the Russell Investments Australian Responsible Investment (RARI) ETF and the BetaShares Global Sustainability Leaders (ETHI) ETF.

Generating a return

While the emerald portfolio isn't aggressive as such, Raiz says it can deliver good returns. That's because stocks with strong environmental, social and governance (ESG) scores have consistently outperformed the global benchmark in the past decade. It favours growing industries, such as technology, which continue to spike, and it rejects businesses that invest in things such as oil, which have underperformed anyway.

As with my super, I want to delve beyond the name of the fund and find out precisely how the holdings are broken down. Raiz doesn't create the funds itself. I start to look at RARI. They've used the positive and negative screening process to give investors access to investments in ESG-focused and responsible practices.

The RARI ETF has holdings in a stack of massive businesses. Unlike my super company, Raiz is transparent about putting my money into this particular fund, and all I have to do is head to the Russell Investments website and download the complete list of holdings. It's a diverse group and I'm surprised to see some of the names on the list. All Big Four banks are there, and they certainly don't strike me as the most ethical businesses to invest in, given the 2019 banking royal commission findings, but I guess they're giving them the benefit of the doubt?

There are some decent companies, such as Medibank Private, which has a corporate responsibility program. Plus there's Transurban, Qantas and a range of media and retail groups. But there are also quite a few mining companies in the mix. I can't see anything that stands out as really ethically progressive.

I have to say, I was underwhelmed, so I got in touch with Brendan Malone, CEO of Raiz. He tells me that after launching in February 2016, they received some feedback from people asking for a socially responsible portfolio. He explains that the emeral portfolio is a combination of ETHI and RARI. 'ETHI makes up the majority – close to 73 to 74 per cent of the portfolio,' he says. 'It's not the greenest thing you'll ever see,' he admits, but he tells me an even better option is on their radar.

ETHI has holdings in businesses that are considered to be 'climate leaders' and have gone through screens that exclude companies with a lot of exposure to fossil fuels or activities that aren't considered in line with ethical investment. This means that companies invested in things such as gambling, tobacco, nuclear energy, animal cruelty, detention of asylum seekers and other human rights issues are not included.

The list of ETHI holdings is just as easy to obtain and this looks better than RARI, so given ETHI makes up the majority of the portfolio I feel a lot more comfortable. It's comprised largely of information technology, healthcare, real estate and financial businesses. No major banks and no obvious investment in fossil fuels.

Brendan suggests that, from an investment perspective, Raiz can provide me with some beginner investment insights that will help me understand how to invest in more sophisticated ways later. For starters, it helps me to make sense of what it means when large sums are 'wiped off the ASX'. 'If you hear that $3.5 billion is wiped of the ASX, that's only 1.2 per cent,' he explains. 'Have a look at your Raiz account and you might only be down 20 cents. It gives you experience in the market to understand what that means.'

He also points out that it can make more financial sense than opening a trading account (which I intend to do shortly). 'Every time you buy an ETF, you have to buy the whole one, you can't micro-invest. CommSec is going to charge you $15 to $20 per trade. When you want the money back they're going to charge you again,' he says.

By contrast, with Raiz I'm only charged a flat rate of $2.50 per month as long as I have a balance of less than $10,000. Then I'm charged 0.275 per cent of my balance if I have more than $10,000 sitting in my account.

'You get experience at an efficient price,' he says.

*

So, for now I decide to hold onto the Raiz app and use it as a micro-saving and education tool. But it's occurred to me that if I want to be truly ethical in my investment decisions and feel absolutely comfortable that the businesses I invest in have good values, I'll have to pick them myself.

A tentative step into ethical shares

Now that I've explored micro-investing, I feel ready to take things further. Although, at this point I still have no idea what I'm doing. So I talk to Kate Campbell, editor of online money education platform How to Money. Kate has a bachelor of business management and also a qualification that allows her to provide general financial information. Kate's mum is an active investor, which provided some early inspiration for her. 'My mum really impressed upon me how important it is to be independent, whether that's through your study, career, relationships or your finances. I always like to have some level of financial control in every situation I'm in,' she tells me.

It was a job early in Kate's career that piqued her interest in investing. 'I started becoming much more interested in investing when I landed an entry-level operations role at an invoice finance startup. It was there that I started to be exposed to money-related conversations on a daily basis, and started asking lots of questions,' she recalls.

While Kate doesn't classify herself as a strict ethical investor, she's spending a greater amount of time getting to know the products and companies that she's investing in. 'Personally, I think the best approach to values-based investing is to pick the companies [shares] yourself,' she says.

As we've seen, many companies across ETFs, shares, super and managed funds all make a great effort to place an ESG/negative screening overlay that suits a broad range of people. 'But it's just not going to gel with everyone's personal views. I'm really interested in companies that are solving problems in both Australia and globally and helping to make people's lives just that little bit better,' Kate says.

Initially, while I'm still getting my head around it, Kate recommends opening up a brokerage account. 'Some of the biggest providers are CommSec and Nabtrade,' she explains. I look at the CommSec option. The Commonwealth Bank isn't a company that many ethical advisers would suggest I do business with, however it's widely viewed as being among the best in share trade tech. There's a lot of information in the app that will help me get a better grasp of the options available to me, so, for now, I open an account, but I don't put any money in it. My aim is simply to use it to build my knowledge base.

How do I set up a brokerage account?

I have to plug in my name, address and phone number and also provide my tax file number (TFN). This is not essential, but if you don't provide your TFN, tax can be deducted from your distributions and earnings at the highest rate. Once you've submitted your application, the broker you've chosen will submit your details to the Clearing House Electronic Subregister System (CHESS), which is the settlement system for Australian Stock Exchange trades.

Next, you'll get a Holder Identification Number (HIN), followed by a CHESS holding statement that documents your purchases. Kate tells me that the HIN is an important one. 'It gives you more security if the brokerage goes belly-up, because you can easily transfer your holdings to another brokerage account,' she explains. If, for any reason, you're not issued a HIN, it's something to think about because you don't have that same protection.

A HIN starts with the letter X and is followed by ten numbers. Any HIN issued with your investment ensures that you own the shares, rather than the broker holding them in their 'sub-register'. Having that direct ownership gives you a bit more control over your assets.

I'm a bit nervous about opening an account. I don't feel confident in my ability. 'There's no harm in opening an account – you can't do much damage. If you're getting started learning, it's quite cool to open the account and put items on your watch list,' Kate says.

Now that I'm set up, I'm ready to explore my options.

What is an ETF?

As mentioned earlier, ETFs are a bunch of shares (sometimes around thirty, sometimes more), bundled together. So that means that for, say, $500, you buy units in an ETF which gives you access to a small parcel of many shares, rather than spending $500 on one individual company share. The advantage is that you spread your risk across several listed companies; the downside, in some cases, is that because the ETF is comprised of so many businesses, it's not unique to your own values, so you may have to choose between spreading risk and staying true to your specific ethical considerations.

ETF providers are companies such as Vanguard and BetaShares. They engage a third-party 'market maker' to ensure the ETF holds its value. 'It's like going to the supermarket. Instead of picking the one fruit you get one of every fruit,' Kate says. So, for example, if you buy what's known as an A200 ETF, you get exposure to the top 200 companies on the ASX with a single trade. Of course, if you're looking to invest ethically, you probably won't want an A200 because so many of the biggest companies are in industries like mining and other dodgy ventures.

The cost of your ETF is usually determined by the net asset value (NAV). The NAV changes depending on the movements of the assets your ETF is invested in. The bid price is provided by the market makers, and they're all in competition, aiming to provide a competitive price.

According to Kate, the market for ETFs has changed dramatically since they became available in 2001. Back then, they were pretty generic, but as the industry has grown, more than 100 ETF options have become available and you can tailor them to focus on the things you value. They don't have to be super-green. They may be tech- or future-focused. BetaShares' Nasdaq 100 ETF, for example, contains a portfolio of 100 tech giants including Amazon, Google and Facebook.

This is a big part of the reason ETFs are growing in popularity. They give you the opportunity to take a gentle step into the share market with a reasonably small investment amount and low fees. The other advantage is you get full transparency. You should be able to access detailed lists of all of ETFs' holdings with ease, so you know exactly where your money is going. Having said that, you might want to do a deeper dive into the ethics of a given holding. Facebook, for example, is heavily scrutinised by some ethical investors due to the way it captures and holds data. If privacy is an ethical concern for you, a company such as Facebook might be a deal-breaker.

It's worth noting that, like any shares, ETFs are susceptible to market shifts and therefore can rise and fall in value. But, ultimately, you'll be hoping for a good return on your investment over time. It's important to read the PDS so you're across all the risks and objectives before you take the leap.

Adding ETFs to your watch list

For an ethical investor, it's not as simple as buying the cheapest ETF or the ones predicted to provide the best return because you need to explore the list of holdings the ETF contains. Kate suggests putting a selection of ETFs on your watch list so you can take the time to see how they're performing and also dig around their holding list to see what they're investing in. Kate tells me to start watching ETFs such as: ETHI, FAIR and VESG. These acronyms are the code you search to find them on your brokerage platform.

We touched briefly on ETHI and RARI earlier, but here's a brief summary of each of these:

ETHI – BetaShares Global Sustainability Leader ETF

Provider: BetaShares

ASX code: ETHI

Top ten holdings: Apple, Mastercard, Visa, UnitedHealth Group Inc., Roche Holding AG, Home Depot, Adobe Inc., NVIDIA Corp, Netflix Inc., Nike Inc.

Overview: This fund has stocks in companies that it deems to be 'Climate Leaders', based on their level of carbon efficiency. They've also passed other screening processes that exclude companies with big exposure to fossil fuels. The screens also reject companies that are exposed to things such as gambling, tobacco, the detention of asylum seekers and other human rights issues.

RARI – Russell Investments Australian Responsible Investment ETF

Provider: Russell Investments

ASX code: RARI

Top ten holdings: Commonwealth Bank of Australia, CSL Ltd, Westpac Banking Corp, National Australia Bank Ltd, Australia and New Zealand Banking Group Ltd, Telstra Corporation Ltd, Transurban Group Ltd, Insurance Australia Group Ltd, Suncorp Group Ltd, Sydney Airport.

Overview: RARI tracks a custom-built index and invests mostly in Australian shares and trusts on the ASX. It focuses on companies with positive ESG features and excludes those that engage in activities viewed as inconsistent with responsible investment practices, such as tobacco, alcohol, gambling, pornography and fossil fuels.

FAIR - BetaShares Australian Sustainability Leaders ETF

Provider: BetaShares

ASX code: FAIR

Top ten holdings: CSL Ltd, ResMed Inc., Suncorp Group Ltd, Insurance Australia Group Ltd, Cochlear Ltd, Sonic Healthcare Ltd, Brambles Ltd, Telstra Corp Ltd, Mirvac Group, ASX Ltd.

Overview: This fund is focused on companies that are considered to be 'Sustainability Leaders'. That means they're chosen based on factors including that they derive more than 20 per cent of their revenue from things such as renewable energy, recycling, waste reduction and water efficiency. It also excludes companies with exposure to many areas deemed unethical, including gambling, tobacco, the detention of asylum seekers, junk food, pornography and a lack of gender diversity on company boards.

VESG – Vanguard Ethically Conscious International Shares Index ETF

Provider: Vanguard

ASX code: VESG

Top ten holdings: Apple Inc., Microsoft Corp, Alphabet Inc., Amazon.com Inc., Facebook Inc., JPMorgan Chase & Co., Johnson & Johnson, Visa Inc., Procter & Gamble Co, Nestlé SA.

Overview: The VESG ETF provides access to several companies that aren't involved in activities such as fossil fuels, weapons, nuclear weapons or pornography. But this is one you might want to dissect in more detail to see if it meets your ethical standards. For me, Nestlé and JPMorgan Chase & Co. aren't the strongest examples of ethical investment.

Which ETFs should I choose?

Well, sorry to be difficult, but it's not for me to tell you. As you can see from these options, there's a range of ethical considerations here. For example, RARI is not really cutting it for me, with all those big banks in their top ten. I don't mind VESG because the management fee is low, and I like Apple and Facebook from an investment perspective, but Facebook has some questionable data and security ethics. Apple also gets poor marks from ethical experts for its contribution to pollution, e-waste and its approach to supply-chain labour rights. Because ETFs aim to give you diversification, they're not going to be perfect.

ETFs might not be for you if you want to be strictly ethical in terms of renewables and corporate governance. However, adding some to your watch list doesn't cost you anything and gives you the opportunity to observe their performance before you dive in.

Ethical admin checklist

 Consider starting with micro-investing. This can be an easy way to understand how investment platforms work without putting too much money in to begin with.

 Research ethical ETFs. If you think you've mastered micro-investing or want to leap straight into ETFs, you'll need to do some research into their contents to decide which ones meet your ethical considerations. As we've seen in earlier investment examples, 'ethical' is a broad term, so you need to do your digging.

 Think about risk and reward. Some ETFs are lower-risk than others. What level of volatility are you comfortable with?

 Start researching brokerage accounts. There are many to choose from. Consider their fees, user experience and the products they have available. In most cases you can open an account for free, but once you start investing you will be charged brokerage fees, so check to see what it will cost to get started. (We'll explore this in more detail in Chapter 8.)

7

Invest Like an Ethical Expert

BECAUSE ETHICAL ETFS AND SHARES are still in their infancy, I decide to talk to others about what they're investing in. That's not to say you should leap in and buy shares in whatever your mate has selected, but by having conversations with other investors, I find out about things that I didn't know existed.

Fiona Crawford is a writer, editor and academic who researches environmental and social issues. Her PhD examined how writers can use multiple platforms to inspire action to address 'wicked problems like climate change'. She's also studying law as a postgraduate so that she can use her research to consider climate change–related lawsuits and be better placed to make her own decisions.

'To meet me, you'd find a polite, introverted, nerdy-looking academic. But I'm sure the funds have me pegged as some sort of radical lefty,' Fiona says.

She has been researching her ethical options for far longer than I have. Like me, Fiona's not a financial adviser but her dedication to investing in things that she sees as aligned with her ethics is admirable.

She's always been environmentally aware. Fiona became a vegetarian when she was nine, and vegan a bit later. 'I have basically forged a career and a life trying to save every animal, tree and insect in between,' she tells me.

She practises what she preaches in all aspects of her life, working with social enterprises including *The Big Issue* and the Homeless World Cup Foundation. Fiona cares for rescue chickens, ducks and cats, and also has bees. She gets around on a bicycle, and has elected not to have children in order to minimise her impact on the planet.

She banks with Bank Australia but, like me, she's using a CommSec account to buy her shares and ETFs. She's looking for a more ethical alternative but it's the best option for her at present.

Finding a super fund has proved difficult for Fiona, who wants an option that reflects her vegan values. 'I've recently been to an ethical financial adviser and am in the process of moving my super to HUB24, and they will manage my super for me and exclude animal testing in medical research,' she explains. HUB24 enables its clients to set up specific exclusions to meet values and needs.

Fiona's ETFs

Fiona has some ETHI shares, but as it stands she doesn't think any ethical ETF is truly perfect. 'The problem is the ETFs aren't ethical enough. I can't control where my money's invested well enough. For instance, I have some ETHI shares but ETHI includes Apple and there are some outstanding questions about the company's transparency and human rights record,' she explains.

In addition, Fiona believes Apple could perform better environmentally by doing things such as standardising their chargers and supporting the right-to-repair movement. This movement is a response to the volume of products going to landfill at the end of a very short lifespan. Apple's phones and computers are quickly superseded by better models and, as a result, contribute significantly to e-waste globally. In Australia, consumer affairs ministers are exploring laws to empower people to repair their phones and electronics to reduce the impact of this waste.

Fiona is vocal about the ETFs that she believes aren't ethical enough. 'I won't invest in the FAIR ETF because it has milk and cheese companies, which doesn't align with my ethical values,' she says. She's contacted BetaShares – the provider of the FAIR ETF – and they've told her they won't be divesting those companies from the product. Advocating for a vegan-friendly ETF is something she's passionate about. 'I've contacted them twice about setting up a vegan ETF. The first time, they weren't interested at all. The second time, they were a lot more receptive. They still haven't set one up, but it seems like maybe they're realising things are shifting,' Fiona says.

Fiona's keeping a close eye on the US-based Vegan Climate (VEGN) ETF, which aims to avoid investment in any company that is engaged in slaughter, cruelty and mistreatment of animals. She hopes Australia will follow suit.

Fiona's shares

Due to the lack of control over what ETFs are comprised of, Fiona prefers to focus on purchasing individual shares in $500 parcels. Many advisers wouldn't necessarily recommend this. Fiona says most experts have suggested minimum investments of $1000 and also told her that she should concentrate on ETFs. Generally speaking, that's because ETFs are cheaper to buy and trade, and they give you access to instant market diversification through investment in a range of companies. But, as Fiona has explained, the trade-off is the reduced transparency and an inability to structure your investments on your personal ethics.

Currently, Fiona's ethical shares are in companies including Mercury (a New Zealand-based renewable energy provider). When she was first getting into ethical investment, Fiona was keen to get her hands on some Beyond Meat shares. Beyond Meat is a plant-based meal company based in Los Angeles.

'I knew Beyond Meat was about to launch, and I knew it was going to be massive, but I was pretty new to investing then – and now it's too expensive to buy,' she explains. At the time, accessing the US stock market was a foreign concept, but now she has a handle on it and she's watching other opportunities.

Bendigo Bank is another organisation that Fiona has chosen to put her money into 'because they don't invest in fossil fuels and because they're supporting innovative banking solutions like Up.' Beyond fossil fuels, Fiona sought to ensure that Bendigo Bank didn't invest in greyhound racing – something else she's staunchly opposed to. At the time, two of the 500 branches provided sponsorship to their local greyhound racing clubs, but those agreements have since ceased.

Fiona is currently looking at the following share options, which she'll consider once she's happy with their ethical credentials:

- BWX Ltd: a natural beauty company with vegan brands such as Sukin, Flora & Fauna, and Zoë Foster Blake's Go-To. Code BWX

- Cleanaway: a waste management service with a focus on recycling. Code CWY

- Costa Group: a horticultural group supplying fruit and veg to retailers. Code CGC

- Sims Metal Management: a metals and electronics recycling company. Code SGM

- Windlab: an Australia-based wind energy technology company developed by the CSIRO. Code WND

- ResMed: a US-based medical company providing cloud-connectable devices for a range of health conditions. Code RMD

Fiona admits that it's unconventional to be so passionate about waste. 'It kind of makes me chuckle, as every time I see a rubbish truck I think they're probably not the most glamorous shares to be buying, but they're very useful companies and ones we're always likely to need.'

She does a lot of research before she commits to investing in individual companies. This is important whether you're investing ethically or not. But in the case of ethical investment, it's even more important to dig beneath the surface – large corporations can go to great lengths to disguise unethical activities going on in the background. So it's up to you to put your private investigator hat on and see what you can find in their financials.

All companies listed on the stock exchange are required to publish an annual report. Just search 'company name + annual report' and it should appear at the top of your results. Sometimes they do cute marketing stuff on the first few pages, like adding beautiful pictures, infographics and inspirational quotes such as 'we are totally committed to building a better world blah blah blah'. I ignore that. The numbers are what matters. These documents are long, so keep scrolling to the financial statements and segment reports.

Don't do it just because it's ethical

If you're just starting out like me, talking to people to find out what they're doing is great, but it could still be worth talking to a financial professional to establish your plan before you do anything serious. I know not everyone can afford to engage a financial adviser, but there are alternatives, such as accountants. There's a big difference between chatting to a friend and consulting an independent expert. Spending money on advice could save you from making costly mistakes.

In Fiona's case, holding the shares for a very long time – more than twenty-five years – is what she hopes will be the key to her success. She has a strong awareness of her risk tolerance and knows that her share values will rise and fall over time. 'I'm also investing because I believe they're the kinds of companies that could and should succeed, so I'd like to help them do that. I don't think doing good and earning money should be mutually exclusive,' she says. 'Obviously, I'm also hoping they'll be worth a fair bit more once the effects of climate change really kick in.'

The ethical spectrum

Fiona is incredibly focused on what I'd call the extreme end of the ethical spectrum. She's passionate about the environment, animal rights and renewables but, as we know, an ethical investment doesn't have to protect the environment to do some form of good.

Alec Renehan and Bryce Leske spent years bantering about the pros and cons of investing in certain companies while they lived in a share house together. They turned their endless chatter into the popular podcast *Equity Mates* in 2017. The pair started their foray into investment from completely different perspectives. Bryce kicked off his investment career in primary school, putting 50 cents a week into a Dollarmites account. 'When I hit $500, my dad put it into a listed investment company. I still own the stocks,' he says.

By contrast, Alec was raised in a family that valued building wealth through the investment in their home. He didn't start buying shares until he moved in with Bryce in 2015. As a novice, he put some cash into Slater and Gordon. 'It went up, and then everything started unravelling,' he recalls. 'I lost 99 per cent of my investment. I couldn't even afford the brokerage to sell it.'

Since then, they've spent a lot of time discussing what a 'good' investment looks like and passing their insights on to listeners. Increasingly, they're exploring ethical investments – a broad and highly contentious issue. 'Ethical is an umbrella term and it has different meanings for different people,' Alec says. Broadly, they know ethical shares perform better than the market average, so there's a lot of interest.

'There's a number of macro factors. Everyone sees the writing on the wall when it comes to fossil fuels – the sector's growth is going to be limited,' Alec points out. But beyond the obvious demise of fossil fuels, choosing ethical funds is about looking for future growth prospects, and these can come in several forms. When we speak, Alec says it's the likes of Apple, Microsoft and Amazon driving the overall performance of the market. Each of these companies has ethical qualities, while also engaging in some unethical practices.

Take Apple, for example. In many respects, the company has made the lives of billions of people better and created incredible opportunities for connectivity. I'm pro-Apple. I'm tapping out this book on my Mac and I've had an iPhone since 2008. Apple has also delivered tremendous dividends to investors as the first American company to achieve a market capitalisation of US$1 trillion, which it hit in 2018. And yet, it has consistently faced serious criticism for its poor supply-chain processes. We're talking unacceptable working conditions in China and human rights abuses, along with significant environmental concerns. While Apple has taken steps to rectify some of these issues, it's still not considered ethical when it comes to manufacturing and working conditions.

'Tech is the hardest and most controversial part of the ethical investing universe,' Alec says. 'These companies can democratise access to information and be a positive societal force, but they can also be unethical in certain areas.'

Alec highlights Amazon workers striking for better conditions because they were paid minimum wage, all while Amazon's share prices soared. He also points to Tesla, famed for its innovative electric cars, helmed by eccentric entrepreneur Elon Musk, who has given shareholders 'governance concerns'. In 2018, he faced a string of vehicle safety concerns and several employment-related lawsuits. In August 2018, without board consultation, Musk tweeted, 'Am considering taking Tesla private at $420. Funding secured.' Dropping a casual tweet about going private in no way met public disclosure standards, not least because he definitely didn't have the funding. The consequences? Musk was removed as Tesla chairman, he paid a US$20 million fine, Tesla also paid a $20 million fine, two new directors were appointed to the board and Musk agreed to have his tweets approved by Tesla before posting in future.

While many of these issues have since been resolved, there is more work to be done at Tesla in terms of both safety and governance. No one wants cowboy-style leadership when their funds are invested in a company, no matter how 'green' its product might be.

Alec also looks to companies such as Facebook 'potentially destroying democracy' by circulating fake news. Then there are concerns about Google's position on privacy.

There's little question that tech has been extremely profitable for investors in the past, and that's likely to continue, but are they ethical enough to invest in when we factor in these issues? Again, this comes down to weighing up what you're comfortable with ethically. 'There's a case that they've made our lives better and they're making commitments around climate change,' Alec says, but adds they all offer reasons for responsible investors to exercise caution. 'Do you eliminate them or weigh it on balance?' Alec asks. 'No one can give you the answer.'

But what's Alec's position? 'I take a negative screen to ethical investing. If it's highly unethical I won't invest in it,' he tells me. That means he doesn't ever invest in fossil fuels or gambling, for example. But for companies that are a little more nuanced, he takes a case-by-case approach. He also suggests that many people will want to apply a more stringent positive screen, such as a commitment to renewables or a board gender diversity level of 40 per cent or more.

We find more murky territory when it comes to some companies, though. 'Energy company AGL is one of the biggest producers of energy from fossil fuels, but also one of the biggest installers of solar,' Alec explains. Then there's Australia's biggest waste company, Cleanaway. Here's a real conundrum. 'They own landfills, but they also own the most recycling facilities. They are the best in terms of driving change, but they're also the worst because they have legacy landfill assets.' As Fiona pointed out earlier, she sees the potential future impact of Cleanaway as valuable. In cases like these it helps to weigh up these considerations. Like big banks, these large organisations have the footprint to make a real difference, often more than the small startups. The question is whether they actually implement meaningful change.

Finally, Alec also suggests looking to the value of investments made in unethical pursuits. 'Exxon spends about US$3 billion a year in exploration – they're unanimously considered unethical,' he says. But compare that to JPMorgan Chase, which might appear innocuous on the surface because it's an investment bank putting funds into all sorts of endeavours. Alec highlights an insidious reality: 'JPMorgan spends about US$60 billion a year in funding projects – that's a tiny percentage of their investments, but it's huge in terms of how much their money is enabling fossil fuels.'

In terms of investing in individual shares, Alec and Bryce point out that you're not locked in with one broker, so you can 'have a play' with a few. These include SelfWealth and IG, which they say are really user-friendly, along with Stake, which makes the investment process clear.

I check out IG. I like it because it allows me to set up a 'demo' account. When I do this, I'm allocated $20,000 of hypothetical shares – a great way to see how I might allocate my spend. I can also practise buying and selling. This is invaluable for a newbie like me.

I also open a Stake account and see that the guys are right – it's really user-friendly. At this point I feel pretty well versed in my brokerage options; now I just need to decide what to buy.

Spreading the love

I'm not nearly as experienced as Bryce and Alec, so I want to talk to someone who has started small and put their funds in a variety of locations to protect themselves from the risk of screwing up. Tash Etschmann fits the bill. At just twenty-four, she's learning as she goes and building quite the portfolio along the way. She shares her financial journey through her Instagram and TikTok accounts, @tashinvests.

Tash moved around a lot as a kid, thanks to her dad's job in mining. 'I lived in Ghana, Nhulunbuy in the Northern Territory, Thailand and PNG before moving to Perth for high school,' Tash recalls. Although she has lived in a diverse range of environments, she says she had a privileged childhood and saw the freedom that having money presented. 'In PNG particularly, all of my friends' families had either a boat or jet ski – the perks of living in small mining towns. We spent most weekends waterskiing, snorkelling or visiting nearby islands.'

But after moving back to Perth, Tash increasingly began to think about the impact of the disparity of income, both in Australia and the other countries she'd called home. 'My grandparents from both sides of my family showed a huge contrast. My nan and pop struggled to pay bills, lived off their pension and were always worried about being able to afford things,' she says. On the flip side, her grandma and grandpa had several investment properties, went on frequent international holidays and were comfortable. In fact, her grandpa is still running his own engineering company at the age of eighty-three.

The first step to reaching her financial goals would be choosing a career that satisfied her need to make money and do work that she valued. 'I decided pretty early on that I wanted the money to be able to do whatever I wanted. I hate the feeling of being stuck, thanks to my parents for exposing me to so much of the world at such a young age,' Tash points out. Inevitably her life experience has shaped her worldview.

Tash opted for a career in occupational therapy. She had learned that she could earn six figures once she worked her way up the professional ladder, but she could also make a difference in people's lives, all while having reasonable work-life balance. Choosing to take her studies slowly has given Tash the opportunity to work consistently while studying, which has played an important part in setting her up for success early. 'When I finished school, I worked multiple jobs during my first year of university,' Tash explains, 'picking up roles as a swimming instructor, a lifeguard and a gig in a sporting stadium. I failed a unit in my first year, which forced me to go part-time. It was actually a blessing in disguise.'

Although the degree took seven years instead of four, Tash worked almost full-time hours in retail and also as a receptionist in an occupational therapy practice. As if that's not enough, she became a qualified divemaster, which means she gets paid to lead snorkelling tours. For the past four years, Tash has held a role as a disability support worker. So although her education has taken longer than planned, she's already got plenty of experience. For most of that time, she juggled various roles simultaneously. 'I was always the person to pick up extra shifts and work all weekend for penalty rates,' she says.

Tash dropped back to one role while she completed her final units of study. She was working a roster of two and a half days on, followed by two and a half days off, then three shifts in which she slept at a group home, followed by nine days off. She was on a base wage of $71,000 and could also choose to work overtime when her study permitted it.

In mid-2021, Tash quit her permanent disability support job and moved to New South Wales for a seasonal snow position working as a receptionist at a hotel. Her new hourly rate dropped to $25 but she spent several months living ten minutes from the Perisher ski fields, and her lifestyle was reasonably inexpensive because her employer provided onsite accommodation and meals. After this, Tash got caught up in lockdowns and ended up moving in with friends in New South Wales until she was able to return home.

Today, she has several sources of income through her occupational therapy work and the marketing opportunities generated through her social media profile. 'I love the freedom of being able to make money online, but find working with people so much more rewarding,' she says. With all the work Tash took on, even while studying, she was well placed to purchase her first apartment, secured with a 20 per cent deposit, two casual jobs and no guarantor. Once Tash had bought her home, she turned her attention to shares.

'Early last year, I started reading books and listening to podcasts to learn more about investing,' Tash says. Her first tentative step involved activating Raiz and Spaceship accounts. She started by using the function that allows her to automatically add $10 to her Raiz account each day. 'I don't notice the smaller amounts at all, it's just on autopilot,' Tash tells me, and it occurs to me that I can do exactly the same thing, so I open my Raiz app and follow her lead, switching on an automatic recurring investment of $10 per day. She also points out that just $10 a day over forty years in an index fund returning 8 per cent equates to more than a million dollars. Hello, yes please! Tash is also putting $100 per week into a separate portfolio with Spaceship, and I look into this too. 'I invest a little more into the Spaceship Voyager app as it's a hand-picked managed fund.' As if that's not enough, she also has shares in a selection of ETFs.

'Paralysis analysis is real, so I just bought whatever I believed was the best at the time and changed my strategy often,' she says.

Initially Tash didn't consult a financial adviser – she took advantage of the plentiful information out there delivered through books and podcasts – but as she grew her wealth, she spoke to a professional to get general advice about insurance, superannuation and her investment strategy.

'Now that I'm investing bigger amounts of money I want a more refined strategy and for someone to confirm that what I am doing is correct. As this is all self-taught I did have small amounts of doubt,' Tash admits. 'As I invest myself, I like to spread my money across lots of products for diversification. I also like the automatic small investments.'

Her Spaceship account now contains $12,800, with $2100 of that figure making up her returns. Then there's $9000 in her Raiz account, with $1600 of that being her return. Tash also has about $7000 in cryptocurrencies, including Bitcoin and Ethereum. In terms of her shares, Tash initially bought ETFs that gave her exposure to a range of different sectors, including emerging markets (IEM), health (IXJ), tech (NDQ) and sustainability leaders (ETHI). While they're not exclusively ethical, Tash has strategically spread her risk, but her interest in ethical options is increasing.

'ETHI is my favourite as it is ethical. It also just paid a 10 per cent dividend, win!' she tells me when we speak. She is also looking into the FAIR ETF.

'I often hear the saying "you vote with your money", which is so true. I just find the "ethical" options are so diversified and there's so many different ways to define it,' Tash adds.

'I now invest with a more ethical focus, including ETFs such as FAIR, ETHI, IMPQ and VESG. I still hold all my previous ETFs but don't actively invest in them anymore. There's a huge difference as to what some companies include in their ethical screens. BetaShares has recently come out with DZZF [their Ethical Diversified High Growth ETF].'

It's all really impressive, but I wonder about the extent to which Tash is still able to enjoy her life while she's young if she's investing all of her money. She told me she values work-life balance and travel, so how does this fit into her financial strategy? 'I love experiences, not things, so this is where I focus my spending.' She's driving the same modest hatchback she's owned since she was sixteen. 'I love investing, diving, travelling, wakeboarding and seeing friends for coffee, so this is what I spend money on. If I want something extra that isn't in my budget, I'll pick up an overtime shift to pay for it,' she adds.

What I realise after talking to Tash is that the most important thing beginner investors can do is identify their values, as well as their financial goals. Having a clear sense of where your money goes, what's important in terms of discretionary spending and how much is left for investment is the key to getting started. That way, you can be confident that you won't need to pull the money out again. As Tash's aim is to invest and hold long-term to get the best results, she's not going so hard that she cuts herself short of funds for day-to-day spending. To avoid this, she documents her spending in a notebook and knows where her funds need to go each week.

'My dream is to work remotely and live somewhere like Bali or Thailand and have enough passive income to do whatever I want,' she concludes.

Ethical admin checklist

 Talk to other ethical investors. This can be really useful when you're trying to understand what the options are. Just remember, they're not giving you financial advice, they're simply telling you what they've chosen to do.

 Explore digital resources. Listening to podcasts like *Equity Mates* or following financial influencers can be helpful. But again, treat these tools as general exposure to what's out there and always do your own research before committing to something you hear about.

8

How to Invest in Shares

SO, NOW THAT WE KNOW the difference between individual shares and ETFs, it's time to start pressing buttons and bringing that share portfolio to life. I have my micro-investments set up, but the process of buying and selling shares still feels pretty overwhelming to me, given that I'm doing it myself rather than going through a financial adviser. I chat to Rebecca Maher, the managing director of Sydney-based firm Proforce. Rebecca explains that there's a number of ways to buy shares, and your preference will likely be dictated by how strong your share market experience is.

Option one: Do It Yourself

Rebecca tells me it's hardly a surprise that I'm feeling overwhelmed by the DIY option, pointing out that you need a fair whack of knowledge to decide what to buy, how long to hold each share and when you should sell or swap. Plus, she says, if you really want to get it right, that often means 'going into one of the research houses and reading research reports, looking at fees, returns and looking at which one is the best one for you and your goals and objectives'.

However, there's a stack of YouTube tutorials that can take you through the process of buying and selling, and plenty of explainer info online.

Queenie Tan makes a living posting financial content on YouTube. 'I started my personal finance journey when I was nineteen. I was at uni and I was working, I had a part-time unpaid internship and tele-marketing job. I made just enough – $400 per week – rent was $250 per week, transport was $50 and whatever was left was for food,' she tells me. Once in a full-time role, she was able to turn her attention to investing. Queenie now holds a range of ethical shares, including Tesla and Beyond Meat. But, she cautions, if you're buying shares in individual companies, there's a lot of research involved. 'I go into a lot of detail when I buy an individual stock. I look at it and ask myself, "Is it in my circle of competence? Do I know enough to make a competent call?"'

Here are some questions Queenie asks herself before she buys an individual share:

- Who are this company's competitors?

- Do I see this company growing?

- Do they have enough cash to weather storms?

- Is their management team growing the business?

- How much does the CEO earn?

- Is the management team ethical?

Queenie is currently investigating companies focused on solar and battery storage but says she's doing more research before she commits.

Rebecca points out that there is a brokerage cost per trade, an additional cost every time you buy or sell, so you'll need to factor that in. That is the fee charged by the broker to complete the transaction for you. Although, 'you can get an account that has capped brokerage like $9.95 per trade', she says. A brokerage account can be a good alternative if you don't want to go through an adviser. Regardless of which provider you choose, Rebecca says, 'you have to make the decision about what you buy and how long you hold it'.

Here are some brokerage platforms and their fees:

- Pearler: $9.50 per Australian trade and $6.50 per US trade (although there is also the option to purchase a range of ETFs that are brokerage-free if you hold them for a year or more)

- SelfWealth: $9.50 regardless of trade size (i.e. it's the same price no matter how many shares you buy)

- CommSec: $19.95 per trade up to $5001

- Nabtrade: $14.95 per trade up to $5000

Option two: See a financial adviser

Rebecca has worked as a solo financial planner and says the cost of giving advice has become prohibitive for advisers due to the amount of box ticking and paperwork. 'It can be 20 hours of work for all the work behind the scenes to say they didn't give you bad advice, to cover themselves,' she says. That means their fees can be prohibitively high for the average Aussie, which can potentially shrink the adviser's pool of customers. 'For anyone who's not got a significant amount of money to invest, it's often not worth their time,' Rebecca says.

It's become so difficult for advisers to operate, largely as a result of tighter rules after the banking royal commission, that reports indicate we would have less than 17,000 advisers in Australia by the end of 2021. That's down from about 28,000 in 2018. The drop in advisers and strong demand is in turn pushing fees up further.

If you do choose to go down this path, you'll provide personal financial information and work with the adviser to establish your goals. Then they will look at a range of products to suit your needs. They'll say, 'You should invest your $5000 or $10,00 this way,' Rebecca explains, and adds that you'll need to factor in their upfront fee as well as a likely ongoing monthly service fee, which could be $200, for example.

The advantage, Rebecca says, is that if you have a question or you want to change your portfolio, the adviser can do this for you. However, for the cost of ongoing management to be really effective, you generally need to be adding money to your portfolio regularly, so that the fees don't counteract your investment.

That said, it may still be worth making some calls to see if you're able to get initial affordable advice. When I was starting my research, I looked to the Ethical Advisers' Co-op, which lists a selection of ethical advisers in each state.

Option three: Get a robo-adviser

A robo-adviser is a mix between do-it-yourself and investment advice, but in this case the advice is generated by an algorithm. Through a robo-adviser service, you input your goals and risk appetite, but rather than do this face-to-face with an adviser, you'll answer a series of questions online.

'Most will have an ethical portfolio. If you tick ethical or socially responsible, they will make a recommendation that you invest in that category,' Rebecca explains. As always, though, don't take any ethical label as gospel. I've come across 'ethical' robo funds that are rammed with questionable companies.

Some examples of robo-advisers include:

Stockspot

Founded by former fund manager Chris Brycki, Stockspot is a response to poor investment advice and high fees. Chris founded the digital platform in order to provide an accessible alternative to traditional financial advice. People with Stockspot accounts are charged a monthly fee based on their account balance.

InvestSMART

Headed up by renowned money experts Paul Clitheroe and Alan Kohler, InvestSMART provides a range of investment options with a $99 per annum capped fee on balances between $10,000 and $18,000. They say that regardless of your bank balance, you won't pay more than $451 in fees per annum.

Clover

Clover provides robo-advice without charging setup, advice or account rebalancing fees. For accounts with $2500 to $9999, there's a flat fee of $5 plus GST per month. Then there's a sliding scale of fees from $10,000 onwards. So, for example, from $10,000 and up, you'll pay 0.65 per cent of your account balance. From $50,000 plus, you'll pay 0.60 per cent and so on.

Option four: Managed funds

Managed funds are similar to ETFs in that 'you're buying units in a pool of investments', Rebecca explains. However, 'a managed fund can't be bought and sold on the stock exchange – an ETF can'.

The upside is that fund managers are quite active in their assessment of the fund's performance. The contents of an ETF are generally static, while a managed fund may change on a quarterly or biannual basis. If something in the fund is not performing, Rebecca says the fund managers might decide 'we're going to boot that and replace it with something else'.

Rebecca points to Australian Ethical's managed funds, which has a minimum investment requirement of $1000, or $500 if you set up a regular investment plan.

Having spoken to Tash, I know that Spaceship's offering is also a managed fund. While I find that it's not strictly ethical when I start investigating, I like its curated approach to its Universe portfolio, with each investment chosen because the company is future-focused. Spaceship is also a very accessible managed fund. Like other micro-investing tools, there is no minimum contribution when getting started. Shortly after I started investigating, Spaceship announced they were opening an Earth portfolio, which would be focused on sustainable and environmental investments. Another box ticked. Earth launched in 2021, and it's now possible to invest funds across more than one of Spaceship's portfolios simultaneously.

Deciding which path to take

It might sound obvious, but after having so many conversations about ethical shares, I have to conclude that the strategy of an ethical investor will be hyper-personal. It can't simply be a case of dumping excess money into shares if and when it suits you. It needs to be part of a holistic approach to investing and the way that it integrates with your life.

I've elected to hold most of the money that I have because I need it for the deposit for my next home, but I have put money in a few places to get started. I'm choosing to do it myself to save on fees initially, but I may seek out financial advice down the track as my funds grow. I've opened a lot of accounts in the name of research, and for the time being I've decided to consolidate my funds so that my investments aren't all over the place.

CommSec Pocket

I download the CommSec Pocket app, which has been designed for new investors who want to buy ETFs. This is not to be confused with the more comprehensive CommSec trading app, which allows you to buy and sell individual shares. There are just seven ETFs to choose from:

- IOZ: Exposure to the ASX 200

- SYI: Thirty companies with a high dividend yield

- IOO: An ETF with a selection of 100 global blue-chip companies

- IEM: A selection of companies in growing economies such as Taiwan, Korea and India

- IXJ: A focus on medical innovation

- ETHI: Exposure to approximately 200 ethical-focused companies

- NDQ: Access to approximately 100 tech companies.

I want to buy units of ETHI, but I also want some exposure to tech. I initially put $200 into ETHI and $200 into NDQ to see how it works. But the Commonwealth Bank isn't the most ethical bank. Although it cost me just $2 per trade when I invest or sell up to $1000 at a time, and is very easy to use, I later find more affordable alternatives for account balances of less than $5000. So I move shortly after I've tried it out and I haven't used CommSec Pocket since.

Spaceship

Inspired by Tash, I also open a Spaceship account. I like the fact that it's a managed portfolio that is reviewed regularly. I choose the Universe portfolio, composed largely of future-focused US-based companies. Like the tech stocks we discussed earlier, some of these companies might not meet your ethical standards, but there are plenty of companies that I like, both from a cultural perspective and for their potential performance. Think Shopify, Etsy, ResMed and Spotify. Then there are progressive local companies such as Nanosonics, an innovative disinfection company; Australian Ethical; and Cochlear. Initially, Spaceship was fee-free for balances of less than $5000. They've since introduced a flat fee of $2.50 per month on balances of $100 or more. I personally see that as a small price to pay for an actively managed fund.

Spaceship has a function that allows me to automatically transfer a set amount each week, so I nominate a figure of $40. Again, Spaceship's not perfectly ethical, but for me it's a start. ETFs and managed portfolios allow me to spread my risk while I'm still learning. But given Spaceship is so new, I take the opportunity to speak to their CEO, Andrew Moore, to learn more about how it works.

In July 2021, Spaceship had more than $1 billion in funds under management. The team developed Voyager almost four years ago. Voyager is a managed fund service with a very low barrier to entry and app-based ease of use. It provides a few managed fund products, each hand-picked by the team's fund managers. I begin with the Universe portfolio that Andrew tells me is put through a 'where the world is going' filter. 'We're looking for forward-thinking companies that will benefit from current trends such as reducing cash (digital payment technology), or QR codes, and also have growth potential. It means there's a tilt towards tech stocks, but Andrew says that technology as a theme is getting worn out, given how few businesses operate without technology these days. 'They're all powered by technology, but they're in a vast array of sectors such as retail, energy, professional services,' he explains.

What I like about Spaceship is the way the managed fund appears to be a bit more active and flexible than an ETF. Switching out their investments and swapping them for better alternatives, much like an experienced share trader would. Andrew explains that ETFs tend to 'track an index'. An index represents a specific group of assets within the share market, such as the ASX 200. 'Once you have an ETF constructed around an index, the stock held is determined by what companies are moving in and out of the index,' Andrew explains.

By contrast, a managed fund like Universe doesn't track a specific index and is made of Australian and international investments. 'In Universe, on a quarterly basis we make an assessment as to what companies could come out and what could come in, testing whether they're meeting the "where the world is going" criteria, and the valuation,' he says.

For a stock to get into the Earth portfolio, it has to be advancing one or more of the UN's sustainability goals; this covers objectives including reducing inequality, achieving zero hunger, enhanced education and more. They'll also apply their 'where the world is going' screen because, Andrew tells me, that's where the returns kick in: the company should be doing good, but it has to be growing too.

When I first see the Earth portfolio, I notice some good companies in there, but I personally would like to see more from the renewables space. 'Some renewables companies are not at the stage where they're meeting our "where the world is going criteria",' Andrew says, but he also says this will change in time. 'Some of those stocks are expensive and their performance has not been great. They need to be good investments too,' he adds.

In 2021, when Earth launched, I moved my funds out of CommSec

Pocket and into Spaceship, so all of my money was in one location. First, I'd much rather be with an independent provider, and second, Spaceship's fee structure is far more attractive. With Pocket I was spending $2 every time I put money in. I'm charged a flat fee of $2.50 per month until I hit $5000 with Spaceship. During that time I also found that Spaceship generally performed well. Finally, I liked having my money in two separate funds (Universe and Earth) in one app.

An absolute Pearler

As I continue to do more research, I know that I also want to hold some ethical ETFs and perhaps purchase some individual shares too, so I look into Pearler.

Pearler was founded by Nick Nicolaides, Kurt Walkom and Hayden Smith in Sydney in 2018 because the trio wanted a really accessible, easy-to-use investment platform. Kurt was interested in money from an early age. He used to count the money in his coin jar each week, and went on to study finance and become an investment analyst. But his ambition was never just about money itself. He has his dad to thank for the advice that continues to drive him: 'Kurt, some people worship money like a religion. They just don't get it. Money isn't the goal. It's the tool that lets you achieve your goals.'

Between his family experiences and his formal qualification, Kurt was often the person his friends would hit up for investing guidance. He recognised the lack of accessible resources and the barriers that young people, in particular, faced. Kurt and Nick worked together. 'Nick and I whinged to each other at work about the difficulties we faced trying to help our friends invest. There was an urgency around learning to invest, and they felt disempowered,' Kurt explains. At this point, Nick was in his early thirties and Kurt was in his mid-twenties.

They saw a gap in the market. 'No broking platform was servicing a long-term investor. They're all trading platforms. That was when we started to look into long-term investing and community-driven marketing.' By that he means that people who use Pearler can set up a profile and display a breakdown of their portfolio. Kurt says the aim is to show that anyone can start investing. 'Someone who's never seen a market screen can make an investment and be confident in that they can set and forget.'

I sign up for a Pearler account, and quickly see that it's definitely intuitive. I create my profile and plug in the key information I need to start investing, including my banking details. I need to supply a form of identification, such as my driver's licence or passport, to get my account approved. Once that's done, I can nominate an investment amount and I can also tick a box to make that amount recurring. I start with $20 per week (because I'm also putting $40 per week into Spaceship). I can choose to build up some funds and invest them when I'm ready. For example, I might wait until I have $500 to buy ETF units. The reason is that it costs me $9.50 per transaction, unless I purchase one of Pearler's forty-three free ETFs. This particular selection of ETFs doesn't have the standard $9.50 fee, provided I hold them for more than a year.

I plan to invest in ETHI, but I'm also interested in investing in individual shares over time. Pearler provides every ASX-listed company, so there's lots to explore. But I need to do more research before I buy individual shares. I ask Kurt about his approach to ethical investing. 'I've started to move some of my portfolio across to ethical. Ethical ETFs have been outperforming standard counterparts. Do I think that trend will last? Probably,' he says.

By September 2021, Pearler had more than 16,000 customers, and shortly after that they hit more than $100 million in funds under management.

Tax time

Now that I have money spread across Spaceship and Pearler, I do need to keep track of any income I make in a given financial year as part of my tax declaration. I speak to Aleks Nikolic, who's passionate about building a diverse portfolio. She shares what she's learned on Instagram and TikTok using her @brokegirlwealth profile.

Aleks is an incredibly savvy twenty-seven-year-old Sydney-based lawyer who has spent the past few years investing across property and shares. 'My parents got divorced when I was younger, and I realised how precarious your financial situation can become overnight. That was a terrifying situation – I thought I was going to have to support my family,' she tells me. 'I realised that it's not enough to just pay off your home loan and pay into your super if you want to achieve financial freedom.'

She started her financial education by looking at investment blogs back in 2017. At that point she was exposed to the 'Financial Independence, Retire Early' (FIRE) movement. Put simply, the theory is that through extreme saving and investing, it's possible to retire earlier than the average age and live off the regular sale of a small portion of the portfolio, or the dividends generated through investment.

Like me, Aleks kicked off her investment journey through micro-investing. 'It was all I could afford at the time. But it helped me understand ETFs, managed funds and volatility in a measured way,' she says.

Today, with years of investment research under her belt, Aleks calls herself an '80 per cent index fund investor'. That means she puts 80 per cent of her funds into ETFs or index-tracking stocks and 20 per cent into growth stocks. Because she's young, Aleks has a long investing timeline and uses a 'buy and hold' strategy, with the aim of generating strong long-term growth and reinvesting dividends. She has shares across CommSec, Pearler and Raiz, so she uses Sharesight to track her investments in one place – a platform that enables users to watch performance and complete tax reporting through its digital portfolio tracker.

'It's integrated with most brokerages, and you can track how much you bought your shares for and track dividend reinvestment,' she says.

If you choose a dividend reinvestment strategy, that means you're taking the money you make on your investments and putting it back into your portfolio. 'The ATO sees dividend reinvestment as income, so you need to account for that income in your tax return,' Aleks explains. 'The income is added to your tax return and taxed at your marginal tax rate – like all other income.'

In addition, if you sell shares over the course of the financial year, you'll potentially qualify for capital gains tax on what you've sold. If you sell a capital asset, such as real estate or shares, you will make either a capital gain or a capital loss. This is basically the difference between what it cost you to buy the asset or share and what you make in terms of profit when you decide to sell. You'll need to report these capital gains and losses in your tax return.

However, Aleks points out it's also possible to reduce your capital gain by 50 per cent on eligible assets by simply holding the asset for more than twelve months. If you sell prior to the end of that period, the whole profit is added to your taxable income and taxed at your marginal tax rate.

'Most major brokerages will issue an end-of-financial-year statement. This includes how many dividends you got as well. I collect the statements and use Sharesight for accounting integration,' she adds.

But what if I don't earn any dividends? 'There's no tax implication if it doesn't produce dividends or you don't sell,' Aleks says.

In the case of micro-investing, you may only generate a very small return initially, and that's okay. But as you build your portfolio over time, the aim of the game is to grow that portfolio and eventually derive income from those investments. Whether you have a small amount to start with or thousands, consistent investing over time can have a huge impact.

For example, an investment of $500 each month for thirty years, with an average return of 8 per cent annually, results in a balance of more than $750,000, assuming you didn't sell along the way. 'That'll outstrip the tax implications,' Aleks concludes.

In addition to tax, I also need to look more closely at my dividend reinvestment plan. That basically means I put any money I make (dividends) back into new shares (reinvestment) rather than taking the cash. For now, we're looking at very small numbers, and therefore the tax I have to pay on the income will be a minuscule amount, but it's something that I need to keep in mind as my portfolio balances rise.

In the meantime, I'm about to get a powerful lesson: the shares will always be there. Sometimes the most impactful ethical investment comes from a relentless desire to make lasting, meaningful change in this bin fire of a world.

And that might mean investing in yourself . . .

Ethical admin checklist

 Decide how you're going to invest. Doing it yourself can be enticing from a fee perspective, but if you're feeling overwhelmed, robo-advice or a managed fund may be a better first step. It's up to you to monitor your comfort levels.

 Look into the ethical options. Sorry to keep banging on about it, but all of these options cover a broad spectrum of what's ethical. There's no quick way around the research. Of course, you want to feel comfortable with the level of risk you're taking on, but you'll also have to think about how ethical each option is.

 Understand the tax implications ahead of time. You might be investing small sums initially, and therefore your tax obligations will be negligible. But even if this is the case, it might be wise to talk to your accountant to gain a better understanding of what happens at tax time.

9

Tangible Impact Investing

IN 2020, *ORANGE IS THE NEW BLACK* actor Yael Stone made the drastic decision to give up her US Green Card and return to live in Australia full-time, arguing that the frequency of her consistent international flights was 'environmentally unjust'.

'We've come to understand that it's unethical for us to set up a life in two countries, knowing what we know,' she said in a video posted to Instagram. 'The carbon emissions alone from that flying – it's unethical. It's not right,' she added.

Stone admitted that she would still sometimes have to fly for work, so she committed to make a significant donation to offset that travel. 'Fifty per cent of the earnings from the next job that takes me overseas goes directly to @feat_artists because it's time for skin in the game,' she wrote on Twitter. Feat is a solar investment movement led by artists and the music industry, based in Australia.

She's certainly put her money where her mouth is, and I reckon it's an impressive call. But she's also in the financially privileged position to do it. With a bit more digging, I discover this is an opportunity that's open to all of us. I spoke to Sydney-based Heidi Lenffer, who founded Feat after running the numbers on the carbon emissions generated by her band Cloud Control's touring.

With the help of carbon analysts, Heidi calculated that fifteen shows, forty-four flights, 16,431 air kilometres and 1843 road kilometres equated to approximately 28 tonnes of carbon emissions. She simply couldn't have that realisation and do nothing about it, so she began to explore ways that touring artists could contribute to a solution.

'We'd stopped touring to write our third record. We were off the road for three years. Once you break the cycle you get to reflect on what you were doing,' Heidi recalls. She'd become increasingly concerned about climate change but didn't know what the creative community could do about it.

'I cold-called anyone who published anything about climate change,' she says. At the time, 'funding had just been cut from science under [Prime Minister Tony] Abbott', and Heidi quickly discovered that many people she spoke to couldn't continue their research. However, the theme of her conversations was consistent: carbon offsetting wasn't the solution. 'We need to make fossil fuels as an energy source redundant and replace it entirely,' came the resounding reply from scientists.

'How can the music industry get behind renewable energy?' Heidi wondered. To find the answer she went down 'a big rabbit hole' of infrastructure investment research, learning how to move money from one industry to another, while also learning how to make this appealing to investors.

Making an impact

Heidi looked into what's known as tangible impact investing. This is where companies and funds invest in projects in which there is a physical outcome. Essentially, the investors raise the capital required to do the work and get a return on that investment. This can work in a range of sectors including low-income housing, education and sustainable agriculture, as well as renewable energy.

'I spent about three or four months chatting to scientists, then I started talking to fund managers and I was introduced to Future Super,' Heidi says. 'Future Super shared a lot of the same goals, and they have a track record of investing with an ethical hat on.'

'The thing that drew me to impact investment was you can use a profit motive for good,' she says. Heidi also saw a dual benefit in creating an accessible opportunity for artists to invest in a project and also help to develop their financial literacy. Heidi saw this as important because many artists have a range of professionals supporting their development and therefore are somewhat naive about money management. 'Artists will go through their careers not understanding the finances behind their operations,' she says. 'They're in a sector that are not encouraged to think of themselves as business owners.'

Eventually, Heidi partnered with Future Super to develop Feat in May 2018. She took 2019 off to complete some studies and pass exams that allowed her, as Feat's founder, to be the company's authorised representative. It officially launched in June 2019. She did most of this while pregnant with her first child, who was born in late 2019.

Feat, through Future Super's fund management, invited artists to invest as much or as little as they liked, which would in turn give them a stake in solar farm development in Australia. 'The minimum we set was $5 to make it accessible,' Heidi says. It didn't take long to attract some iconic names, including Midnight Oil, Regurgitator and Vance Joy. Heidi had a hit on her hands. Feat quickly attracted interest from high-profile people outside the music industry too. Today, Feat is 'led by the arts industry for everyone', Heidi says. Which means I'm able to invest via a few clicks on Feat's website, which I intend to do.

In less than a year they'd raised $5 million in funds and anticipated returns of 5.2 per cent, and there's an option to reinvest or withdraw returns annually. The first farm bankrolled by Feat is the Brigalow Solar Farm in south-west Queensland. It's expected to be powerful enough to service 11,300 homes for thirty years.

'Business is quite creative, it turns out. It's something that's achieving real outcomes. Seeing it rippling through the community is rewarding,' says Heidi.

Equity crowdfunding

If you're not ready to build a formal share portfolio, I have good news. Times are changing and it's possible for you to put a small sum into a business you believe in, through equity crowdfunding.

Crowdfunding isn't new, but equity crowdfunding was only officially legislated in Australia in 2018. At that time, ASIC gave Australian Financial Services licences to some innovative platforms. The concept gives private businesses and public unlisted companies the chance to secure funding by offering a share in their company to anyone who wants to invest. Historically, startups and small brands had to apply for investment through venture capitalists and high-net-worth (aka ultra-wealthy) people. Now, they can gather up to $5 million a year through equity crowdsourcing. And the benefits are twofold. Regular people can invest in the raising of capital, in some cases by contributing as little as $50.

The technical term for this concept is crowd-sourced equity funding (CSF). Here's the catch for you as an investor – returns are generated if the company you've invested in exits through a trade sale, initial public offering (IPO) or share buyback. It means you're taking a speculative risk, but the payoff is the possibility of high returns if the company achieves its objectives.

*

If you're looking to make a quick buck, equity crowdfunding might not be for you. That's because these types of businesses can't be traded on public exchanges, so you can't necessarily sell if you change your mind or need to get the money out. But the low barrier to entry might be appealing. As is the fact that it's all above board. Under the legislation, each company has to provide an offer document with key information, which allows you to do your research before you throw your money at it. At the very least, it's more secure than flicking a fifty at your entrepreneurial mate who wants you to invest in their next big idea.

Choose your investment

As a result of the change in legislation, a bunch of interesting platforms are popping up to provide equity crowdfunding services. Take Birchal, a tool that allows you to pick a brand you're interested in and throw some cash at it. In January 2010, it was one of the first ASIC-approved platforms in Australia; it's the brainchild of the founders of Pozible – one of Australia's most recognised crowd-funding platforms, where several charities, entrepreneurs and arts initiatives have raised funds through small pledges – so you can rest assured that they know what they're doing. I spoke to Alan Crabbe, founder and CEO of Pozible, who talked me through the Birchal process.

Essentially, through Birchal, companies can now facilitate a promotional call-out to prospective investors (that's anyone, including you and me) and receive investment funds through the platform. To invest in a chosen company, they need to have an offer live. They might also be running an expressions of interest campaign. 'You can view the offer document and consider the investment opportunity. There's quite a lot of details about the business, missions, objectives and their financials,' Alan explains. They also have to set a minimum and maximum time frame they want to raise the funds in.

It's not just easily accessible for newbie investors like me, Alan says; it also provides opportunities for emerging brands like never before. 'We think these companies and brands can hopefully build a community and accelerate their growth. It's a larger audience of people that will engage with that company and hopefully be able to drive the amount of money required,' he says.

Indeed, when a group of people consciously choose to invest in that specific business because they believe in what it's trying to achieve, there's a lot of potential. While not all of the businesses seeking funding on Birchal will have a strict sustainable or ethical standpoint, most have qualities that appeal to their audience's values. 'Ethically, it's quite important for a modern consumer brand to be considering themselves to be socially and environmentally conscious – we do see certain audiences engage with that,' he says.

He points to Seabin, which is among the most ethical options, with live offers open when we speak. The company manufactures floating garbage bins designed to capture plastic and other waste to protect our waterways. 'This is a perfect case of a consumer company scaling up, and the community supporting it.' Alan says.

I explore the range of options on Birchal and come across some great companies. For example, there's Real Good Honey, which supports beekeepers and raised $789,924.90 through 538 investors in an offer that closed on 13 July 2021.

Alan explains that I can click 'I'm interested' in any company that takes my fancy. 'You're making the application to acquire shares; once the company meets the minimum target, the payment is then processed. In return for that investment you get the shares in the company and any other investor awards,' he tells me. But because I'm putting my money into private companies, rather than buying shares in a publicly listed company, my shares are not tradeable. Alan explains that the way to get my return is through an 'exit offer', which becomes available if the company is successful.

Sustainable style

If you were to put together a list of people who spring to mind when I say 'socially conscious fashion', I'm quite confident actor Liam Neeson wouldn't be included. But for James Bartle of Outland Denim, it was Neeson's role in the film *Taken*, and its focus on human trafficking, that inspired James and his wife, Erica, to think about what they could do to drive change through their work.

After seeing the film, James travelled to Asia with an anti-trafficking rescue agency to witness the reality of human trafficking. 'It was there that I saw the problem. I saw a young girl for sale, and it rattled me enough to want to help,' he recalls.

The pair started their business five years ago and focused on high-quality sustainable denim jeans, but their simultaneous aim was to engage seamstresses and staff living in countries where they are exposed to exploitation. Once employed by Outland, they are paid a proper living wage and are also provided with an education program that includes household budgeting, language, self-defence and health.

They started working with five seamstresses in Cambodia, and today they have more than 100 staff – many whose lives have changed significantly. James says it's having a remarkable impact, citing one woman who 'built a home after living under a plastic sheet and also bought her sister back from someone who owned her'. He says this has a positive flow-on effect in the community too. Not only are the women workers empowered, but they're also learning innovative garment construction techniques, including the use of a 'green' oxidising agent that requires 80 per cent less chemical use, 20 per cent less energy and 65 per cent less water than traditional alternatives. It was important to create environmentally friendly denim and help to sustain the lives of the workers employed. 'Then we could say we developed a genuinely sustainable product,' James says.

The business kicked off with a round of private investment, which has allowed them to invest in their own facilities to ensure quality control. But in line with its values, they moved to equity crowdfunding. 'Many people don't have the money for an exciting investment opportunity that could turn a healthy profit,' he explains, but through crowdfunding Outland engaged its community of consumers, offering them a chance to own their share with a minimum investment of $250.

During the campaign in early 2020, 1012 people invested, raising a total of more than $1.3 million dollars – not bad considering it came at the peak of the pandemic onset panic. But how do all these people get a return on their investment? 'I don't know how we're going to manage 1000 people's expectations,' James admits, but says it will come down to regular communication. 'If they don't get a return, we haven't done our job,' he adds.

But with much of their money going into research and development, along with revolutionary technologies, he's getting interest from other brands who'd like to access the facilities. Outland is already working with New Zealand-based, high-end brand Karen Walker, and is expanding the opportunity to more brands, which will inevitably help the business to grow, in turn giving its community of investors the returns they hope for.

Queensland-based forty-one-year-old Jason Harris found out about the opportunity to invest in Outland through some friends. It was his first ethical impact investment, and he contributed a sum of $8000. He says it was easy to go through the process, 'just like online shopping'. He's expecting a return within three years, though when we speak it's too soon to tell what this might look like. In the meantime, as an investor, he receives regular updates from Outland via email and Facebook. Jason says:

The investment for me was not just an ethical issue, it was also financial. If we are to find solutions for ethical concerns globally they must be solutions where there are more winners than losers. Seeing the outstanding growth of Outland, despite the fact that they have not had a concentrated push into any market, means they have a bright future. The foundations are there.

Becoming a force for change

Impact-investing opportunities are not limited to environmental causes. There's a stack of passionate people out there building impact-investment causes linked to their personal values. Property developer Greg Cree hadn't planned to get into impact investing, but the 2011 Brisbane floods set him on a new path. Greg, among others, was involved in a support program in Ballymore, Brisbane, when the floods hit.

In the days immediately following the height of the floods, Australians watched the events play out. 'Kochie was there, all the press was there for a while,' he recalls. But soon enough media interest subsided. 'When they left, we went on for ten weeks doing what we were doing.'

'These people didn't do anything wrong; they simply had a place where the water came,' he adds. It was at this time that Greg realised communities impacted by disaster needed longer-term plans that weren't reliant on government investment and fundraising. He began to research the non-profit space as well as structures for community programs. 'Everyone says, "You're a filthy property developer, you won't become a charity,"' Greg remembers.

Greg set his sights on developing an investment fund that did more than simply asking for charitable donations. With the model he created, he'd be able to sustain the concept of affordable housing, while giving those who invested a return too. He points out that housing affordability in Australia is a significant problem. If you're spending more than 30 per cent of your household income on your living arrangements, then you're in housing stress. He says that at the vulnerable end of the market, some people are spending 80 per cent of their income to secure a roof over their head and can't break the cycle.

The concept, Housing 4 Change, uses an impact-investment structure, donations and partnerships to provide affordable housing in his community. The homes that are built are designed for either rental or purchase, for those facing adversity. Their philosophy is 'doing good while doing well', meaning investors can make meaningful change for those in need while also deriving a return from their investment, by ensuring each development turns a profit. With the aim of providing housing solutions, Greg's team has worked to raise equity through private investment and donation to finance the medium-density houses, townhouses, and house and land projects. The priority is to accommodate people on waiting lists for social housing, people with disabilities, vulnerable women and the elderly.

'It's not been easy, people rubbished me,' he says. But a decade later he's proved the naysayers wrong. Greg believes the beauty of impact investing is working independently of government bodies. 'The cost of administering reporting for the government costs a lot,' he points out. Working privately, he has the freedom to put those funds into project work.

In 2020, he started a new fund dedicated to bushfire recovery. He explains that there were many issues that came with donations made to the cause – funds became tangled in government and charity administration, slowing down the process of distribution and making it unclear where individual donations actually ended up. To invest in this fund, people are invited to invest amounts starting from $5000, for a minimum of three years, with an anticipated return of 6 per cent per annum.

'I feel I've been given this task, to start a movement,' Greg concludes.

Starting small

Rhianna Knight, a twenty-nine-year-old Melbourne-based fashion designer, completed Fashion Design at RMIT and interned at a couple of major brands, including Country Road. Later, she took another internship at a snowboarding apparel company. It wasn't the dream gig, but it was a small business in which she was able to transition to a full-time role and gain exposure to the entire manufacturing and retail process – something she mightn't have seen at a larger fashion house.

'By the end I was responsible for design production,' Rhianna says, which meant she was overseeing everything from garment sketches through to sourcing swing tags. In the few years Rhianna worked in this role, she also visited manufacturers, worked to improve supply-chain programs and began to explore ethical manufacturing processes. It was an unusual amount of responsibility for a recent graduate, but it gave Rhianna a clear sense of what was required if she was to develop her own line of clothes.

Rhianna's career-defining light-bulb moment didn't happen at work, though. It happened on a trip to Patagonia, hiking up mountains and exploring canyons – it seemed no matter which way she looked there were uninterrupted views of natural beauty. That was unless she looked down at herself. 'I was wearing really ugly clothes,' Rhianna laughs. It wasn't just that the style wasn't to her taste. 'I felt really self-conscious about what I was wearing. It was a regular synthetic fabric, derived from oil.'

There was something incredibly jarring about being passionate about the outdoors and the natural environment while being clad in threads that were so uncomfortably human-made. 'I'm going to start my own brand,' Rhianna decided. The aim was to find the sweet spot between style, sustainability and function. Garments would be made from recycled and non-conventional fibres. No single-use plastics would be used in the delivery of goods to customers' homes. Back in Australia, she got started on the planning of the brand: Team Timbuktu.

In late 2017, Rhianna started a crowdfunding campaign using a platform called Indiegogo to source enough funds to get cracking. 'I made $21,000 in the first production run,' she recalls. Given her industry experience, she was confident about her ability to design and produce a sustainable activewear line. 'Aesthetically I knew what I wanted,' she says. It was a case of exploring textile and manufacturing options.

In the past three years, Rhianna has sought to consistently improve her products as she learns. Even delivery has evolved – orders were once placed in cardboard envelopes, but now they use compostable mail bags. In terms of textile design, Rhianna initially used Econyl, a recycled fabric produced from industrial plastic, fishing nets and other waste. Now she creates her leggings and crop tops using only plastic bottle waste. It's 73 per cent recycled polyester derived from the plastic, mixed with elastane, which is required for the stretch factor. According to Rhianna, plastic bottles can be turned into garments surprisingly easily. First, the caps and labels are removed, they're sterilised, and then they're 'melted down to a Corn Flake size and then to a Rice Bubble size,' Rhianna explains. Once it's that small, it's then further refined into the fabric. Finally, prints or dyes are added. Unless people are explicitly told, Rhianna says, 'the end consumer has no idea it's a recycled fabric'.

She looks for materials and manufacturers that are Global Recycle Standard (GRS) certified. The GRS operates internationally and verifies working conditions and environmental processes in spinning, weaving, knitting, dying and printing around the world. Like many designers who engage manufacturers in other countries due to the cost of local production, Rhianna physically goes to the locations –

because it's not enough to design ethical garments, they should be made ethically too.

'I see the office and the factory floor,' she says, before adding, 'There's still trust involved. It's about finding the people who can grow with you.' Rhianna is careful to ensure the certification documents exist.

It's all very impressive, but how lucrative is it? 'We're still not profitable,' Rhianna admits. 'It takes effort to grow and scale.' A non-sustainable fashion brand could potentially scale up its production, output and therefore profit much faster than she can. 'Because I've decided to go "best practice", that impacts my scale,' she points out. What she means is she's not using the cheapest textiles or manufacturing processes, which in turn makes her product more expensive than 'fast fashion'. And, ultimately, she must complete smaller production runs to fit within her budget.

But she's not rushing to build a company with fifty staff and lightning-pace production cycles in order to speed up her financial viability; the impact of the work and the cultural significance holds as much value as the profit and loss statement. Rather than building a brand fast, Rhianna is taking the time to explore the ways in which she can continue to do good work while improving her cashflow, explaining the goal is to achieve 'financial sustainability'.

Still, as challenging as it's been, Rhianna is happy to be investing in her own vision and driving change. 'If you look at how many clothes are made each year, a change in just 1 per cent will have a huge ripple impact,' she believes.

And she's right. Just talking to her has me thinking about the amount of clothes sitting in my wardrobe that go unworn most of the time. The cheap T-shirts that were most likely made by people working in intolerable conditions for inadequate wages. I immediately commit to make far more considered fashion purchases in future.

In the short term, Rhianna is working to get to the point where she can hire a handful of in-house team members, so she can focus on her strength and leave the likes of marketing and legal to others. That means getting the cashflow to the point where she can justify the cost of a few salaries but, in time, additional private investment funding might be needed to support the growth of her business.

Funding your sustainable business idea

It's one thing to have a killer idea for a sustainable business, it's another to have a flow of income to make your goals achievable. This is where venture capital, angel investors and business grant providers can come in. With a strong business plan pitched to the right investor at the right time, you might be able to secure the startup funds needed to launch and sustain your business.

Venture capital is not a new concept. Private investment firms are the undercurrent of many successful companies. The fact is: you need money to make money. Investors generate returns through management fees or agree to take a percentage of your company's profits. The advantage, of course, is the initial cash injection that gets you up and running.

While venture capitalists and private investors are ultimately businesspeople seeking to profit from their investments, there are many with the simultaneous objective of backing entrepreneurs who have an idea that might enhance our future.

I jump on a call with Bec Milgrom, who with her siblings runs a private investment company called Tripple. The siblings run Tripple with a 'force for good' philosophy, and a desire to create a better future for people and the planet.

'We are borrowing the earth from future generations. Not responding to climate crisis and inequality is a business, environmental and human risk,' Bec tells me.

And she's right. Next-generation investors are making carefully considered values-based decisions in a way we've never seen before, due to the environmental, social and economic catastrophes they've been exposed to as they've grown up, and their ability to force change is immense. Trillions of dollars are currently being transferred into the hands of family successors. It's actually the most significant wealth transfer in history.

According to the 2019 Wealth-X Family Wealth Transfer report, it's estimated that in the 2020s alone, US$8.8 trillion will go to America's gen X and millennials, US$3.2 trillion to Europe's next-gen investors and US$1.9 trillion to Asian recipients. 'That's going to come with a shift in thinking,' Bec explains. Yes, it's an extraordinary amount of money, but in the pockets of those with a social and environmental conscience, it has the potential to change global financial models.

Presently, there is a remarkable disconnect between economic objectives and the environmental impact of business pursuits. 'It's an invitation to wake up,' Bec says. 'Beyond the obvious environmental and social reasons not to invest in fossil fuel industries, we also don't see them as long-term winners in a low-carbon world, so why would we invest in them?'

Bec is not alone in this thinking. Astute investors have identified opportunities in burgeoning and essential industries and place emphasis on putting funds into ventures that are not only important for the global population but have huge potential for growth.

'Community food hubs are inevitable in the future,' Bec says, outlining just one example that old-school investors wouldn't have entertained. The Tripple trio, when contrasted against legacy investors, are seeing investment through the lens of their relative youth. They're considering the rise of democratic lending that benefits societies and economies in the long term, as well as the numbers on a profit and loss statement. In choosing the businesses they will invest in, or provide grants to, they are looking for inspired leaders, with ideas that target a specific problem and deliver a high-impact, sustainable solution. 'We're looking for that sweet spot of exceptional founders creating great solutions to tackle some of our most pressing challenges,' Bec says.

She admits that they don't have all the answers – no one does. 'At a minimum we're trying to move the needle to better, not perfect, solutions,' Bec suggests. 'The goal is a thriving future for everyone.'

Tripple is not unique in its approach to ethical investment. There are several venture capitalists and private investment firms focused on specific aspects of the ethical spectrum. Chances are there's an investor with an interest in your niche. Clean tech, energy, environment, waste management, healthcare, agri-tech, carbon mitigation, social impact – there are funds that want to support innovation in these spaces right now.

Ready to raise investment funds for your ethical business?

Ten tips from Tripple

1. *Own your why:* What's your story? What makes this the business you can't wait to build, and why are you the right person for the job?

2. *Know your challenge:* What is the big problem you're trying to solve? Why is it important?

3. *Know your solution:* What is your business model? What makes you unique? How do you plan to grow? What major barriers do you anticipate in the short and long term, and how will you address them?

4. *Get to know the market:* Who are your key competitors? How are you different or adding value to the market as a whole?

5. *Build a team to stack the deck:* Anyone can have ideas but execution is what makes things happen. Who is on your team today? Why are they right for this job? What are your capacity gaps and hiring plan?

6. *Work out how much money you need.* And what are you going to do with it? With your current staff, hiring plans and expenses, how long can you sustain your business?

7. *Become a networking superstar:* Get in front of as many people as you can, and ask for advice and warm introductions as early as you can. You should expect to talk to a lot of investors before you find the right match.

8. *Find out what the investors want.* Working out what makes your investors tick and whether you fit into their criteria before you meet with them will make your pitch stick.

9. *Find your tribe:* Surround yourself with people who know what you're going through, and connect with other founders who are a couple steps ahead of you on the journey.

10. *Nail your pitch:* Pitch first to investors who you are okay with not winning before you pitch to your most important leads. Practice and confidence make perfect!

Ethical admin checklist

 Choose your investment. Your imagination is the limit when it comes to choosing the kind of impact you'd like to have.

 Consider the liquidity of your investment. If you're putting funds into a platform such as Birchal, keep in mind that your shares aren't tradeable, and returns may differ from investment to investment. Read and understand all the terms and conditions.

 Starting your own ethical business? This can take time and a lot of capital to get off the ground. Research business models and how you'll establish cashflow.

10

Becoming a Speculative
Ethical Investor

HOW FUNNY WOULD IT BE if it turned out cannabis could save the world?

Actually, it's not a joke. And, no, I'm not high. This is a very real possibility. In fact, the proof is growing on farms around Australia right now.

Entrepreneur Richard Evans didn't expect to end up in the business of hemp, but he's certain that he's developed a revolutionary formula that's going to disrupt farming, housing and the environment all at once. Back in 2008, he was impacted by the global financial crisis and forced to close his UK-based property development company. While contracting at a firm shortly after, he worked with a man who took him to a farm in England and showed him a crop of industrial hemp. 'He said, "This is going to change the world,"' Richard recalls.

Curious about this apparently magical plant, Richard conducted his own research, and the potential use of this material became somewhat of an obsession. In 2010, he took a trip to Australia to visit some friends in Coogee. *Could you imagine how much hemp we could grow here?*

he thought. A week after his trip, he was applying for a visa. Richard ended up in Perth, which was in the throes of the mining boom and attracting a solid British expat community. It took years of research, development, networking and discussions with farm owners before he had the experience and the knowledge to launch his business MIR-RECO, which is focused on processing hemp and developing products with the material.

When we speak in 2020, he's just about to launch his prototype hemp house.

How a superfood grows into a home

Hemp is enjoying a renaissance after being all but banished from society in the late 1930s. The use of hemp goes back thousands of years – documented way back in 2800 BC.

By 1619, the hemp industry was thriving, particularly in the United States. In fact, there were laws ordering all farmers to grow the stuff. It was also made legal tender that could be used to pay taxes. But by the 1930s, a few wealthy folks in the oil, petrochemical and pharmaceutical businesses, who were under threat due to ongoing advances in hemp manufacturing, started a smear campaign claiming that all products containing cannabis – including hemp – were dangerous and should be outlawed. In actual fact, hemp was a serious threat to their plastic and synthetic material businesses.

In 1937, the US Congress passed a bill prohibiting the growth of these products. Falling into step with the United States, Australia followed suit. The remarkable thing is, prior to the ban, Levi Strauss was making jeans out of hemp and Henry Ford designed a car comprised largely of hemp materials that also ran on clean hemp energy. You have to wonder where we'd be today if the grubby oil merchants hadn't been successful.

In April 2017, the ban was finally lifted, creating new opportunities, demand and exciting prospects.

According to Richard, the great thing about hemp is the natural fast pace of production. 'We've just harvested a crop in seventy-nine days. The climate in Australia really supports hemp production.

'There's a new industry that's ready to explode because of the sheer volume that we can grow with sun and water,' he adds. And that's exactly what he intends to do. The rise of the hemp industry has the power to reinvigorate farming in this country. Especially if it's used to build sustainable homes.

Richard's hemp house, which took more than three years to design, is more than sustainable, though. Hemp can store carbon dioxide. His dwelling stores it in the floors, walls, partitions and roof. With a glazed window system, Richard says, 'it's basically going to create its own power'. That power is sent to a lithium battery, where the energy is stored. The best-case scenario, Richard claims, is that it's possible to 'develop a carbon bank and decarbonise the construction industry'. In short, that means people who own hemp houses could stand to profit from carbon trade agreements.

It's a lofty goal, but Richard has the support of the West Australian government.

For now, the materials are made using a liquid-based non-synthetic polymer and constructed using a pre-fabrication method. But, in time, Richard plans to be in a position to pop the liquid into a 3D printer and 'print' houses onsite. This might seem absurdly futuristic, but it's already happening in other parts of the world. In 2018, a house in Italy was 3D printed with a concrete-like material comprised of recycled demolition debris. It was constructed within a week. In 2019, a two-storey, 640-square-metre commercial building became the biggest 3D-printed construction in the world. It was made using technology by Apis Cor, a leader in 3D construction. Experts predict that as this technology becomes increasingly sophisticated, it could significantly reduce the cost of housing.

In Australia, it's the hemp component that could be a real game-changer, though. As if it's not impressive enough that it's sustainable and stores carbon, Richard and his team have also tested the combustibility. 'The tests show you cannot burn our hemp houses. You cannot burn carbon dioxide. It's another string to the bow,' he says.

I have to say, I'm pretty captivated by hemp and the potential for its growth. I begin to look into listed hemp-focused companies and seek out possible opportunities to buy shares.

What's a speculative stock?

Because the hemp industry is so new, it's also volatile. New companies could go through the roof in value, but they could also collapse without warning. So it's obviously not something I'm going to put my life savings in, but I'm definitely curious.

For now, I add The Sustainable Nutrition Group (ASX code: TSN), a hemp-focused farming and retail company, to my watch list to see how it performs while I do more research. TSN is what people might refer to as a speculative stock. If I was to invest, I would be what's known as a speculative investor. Traders quite literally use speculative stocks to speculate. The trader may have some insight into this particular stock and believe that it has significant potential. Often, speculative stocks have comparatively low prices compared to blue-chip stocks, but they're also pretty risky. They're often stocks in emerging markets that might be relatively unknown or understood. But the risks associated with this type of investment are also what's attractive about them – they could generate much higher returns than the benchmark.

When I speak to financial adviser Alex Jamieson, he suggests that 5 to 10 per cent of my investment portfolio should be in a 'speculative bucket'. This means I'm using a small amount of my funds to take risks on shares that are more volatile than most others. He highlights Tesla as an example: in 2019, the share price was changing constantly. 'A company that's in its infancy can typically move around 50 per cent through the course of the year,' he explains.

While risk on speculative stocks is high, there's also potential for great gains. However, he urges me not to go overboard because I'm excited by the prospect of a particular stock type. 'You don't need quite as much exposure,' he says, and adds, 'You want to manage a risk that doesn't railroad long-term objectives.'

Pot stocks

Alex tells me that Canada is leading the way in the cannabis sector, and says that there are some ETFs that I might consider. But before I do that, I need to understand a bit more about the market. That's because sometimes people will get really excited about an emerging market, but without much history of returns it can be hard to predict how it will perform.

But that's not necessarily going to be the case with emerging ethical markets. That's because there is a genuine need for many of the companies producing goods and services in the environmental and social spaces. As demand grows, there's potential for the share price to rise. On the flip side, when a market is 'immature' there's a chance these new companies could fall over or be displaced by a better option. So you need to keep a close eye on what's happening. I see speculative investment as a bit like gambling – you're backing a long shot in the hope that it races home to the surprise of more conservative pundits.

In the case of cannabis, stock prices soared in 2019 but then slumped later in the year due to a few factors, including changing regulations.

Many investors took advantage of that decline. According to *The Australian Financial Review*, activist investor Merchant Group bought an 11.4 per cent share of AusCann for more than $5.4 million in late 2019. Arguably a good buy, given that it was trading at 32.5 cents per share around that time, after trading at up to 96 cents per share a year prior.

There could be massive potential for hemp and cannabis stocks. Not only because there's huge scope to physically grow it here in Australia, but because there are so many industries that can use this resource that some people are calling it 'green gold'. From medicine to food and housing, this natural resource really could be a game-changer.

Speculative ethical investments at a glance

We've already discussed hemp in some detail, and while that's the area that's piqued my interest, you might have other markets you'd like to explore.

Healthcare

The need for quality healthcare will only continue to grow as our population expands and ages. The opportunities to invest in healthcare are broad. Perhaps you're interested in hospitals, mental health, biotechnology or aged care. According to the Australian Bureau of Statistics, by 2057 there will be approximately 8.8 million older Australians, comprising 22 per cent of the population. By 2097, there'll be 12.8 million, or a quarter of the population, aged over sixty-five. So it stands to reason that we need huge investment in healthcare.

While the sector has generally performed well, some experts argue that there are shares available at inflated values due to their relative scarcity. In addition, some investments in the Australian market are highly speculative because of their emerging technologies and potential to fail.

A good way to expose yourself to emerging healthcare stocks is by investing in established global corporations or considering health-themed ETFs, such as the BetaShares Global Healthcare ETF. Having said that, there are many pharmaceutical companies in there, so you need to decide just how ethical you want to be.

Technology

Obviously, the pickings in the technology sector are rich. In the United States, technology shares are among the leading investments. These include Apple, Amazon, Google's parent company Alphabet Inc., Facebook and Netflix. There's a stack of exciting emerging subsectors too, including sex technology, artificial intelligence and virtual reality.

In Australia, though, we're not seeing the same results as in the United States. We have some interesting players, including software development giant Atlassian, which is listed on the US stock exchange, and Afterpay (recently acquired by digital payment firm Square), which has performed well in recent years and expanded into the US and UK. But tech stocks still make up a small percentage of the ASX-listed investment options.

So, again, ETFs provide good general exposure without putting all your eggs in one basket. An example is NASDAQ 100, which has holdings including Microsoft and Facebook. If you're into cyber security, check out the BetaShares Global Cybersecurity ETF (ASX: HACK), and if you're curious about robotics consider the ROBO Global Robotics ETF (ASX: ROBO). The Asian technology market also provides some good prospects. If this is of interest, you might want to explore the BetaShares Asia Technology Tigers ETF (ASX: ASIA)

Agriculture

No matter how the world changes, we will always need food and water. But the way in which we get our nutrition is increasingly changing in line with values-based diets. Take, for example, US-based Beyond Meat, which produces plant-based meal substitutes that are designed to replace chicken, beef and pork. Its stock values skyrocketed after its initial public offering (which is essentially where a private company lists on the stock exchange) in mid-2019.

In Australia, agricultural businesses could support strong economic growth in the future, given we have a reputation for growing food safely and sustainably. We also have a robust supply chain and a diverse range of climates that support the growth of niche ingredients through to mass market crops. We're also making great strides in agricultural technology – agri-tech for short. One example is Roots Sustainable (ASX: ROO), which is focused on technology that heats and cools crop roots to achieve optimum temperatures to deliver fast produce yields, even when specific items are out of season.

Transport

As populations swell, moving people around will continue to be a priority for governments and urban planners. Increasingly, innovative countries are also exploring ways to do this sustainably. Think battery- and ammonia-powered boats and electric buses. Tesla is the obvious early investment in electric vehicles, but most motor companies are working on electric options now. Then there's Enel X, which has rolled out fleets of electric buses in locations around the world.

As our population grows, the ways in which we move people efficiently and sustainably is likely to change. Autonomous electric vehicles ferrying you to and from your destination while you kick back and watch Netflix? It's not as far away as you might think, so keep an eye on the players that are driving change.

Alternative speculative investments

Perhaps, instead of investing in Tesla, you buy one. Yes, most financial advisers will tell you that a car is a depreciating asset, but who's to say an early Tesla model won't be a collector's item some day? History tells us that classic cars become collector's items. Although, given there's a starting price of around $60,000 for a base model, there are a few other ways I'd invest that money before buying a flashy car.

Similarly, art could have the dual benefit of looking lovely on your wall and rising in value simultaneously. Is art ethical? Well, perhaps not in the blatantly obvious way that renewable energy is, but if you want to support the arts sector, you might see great value in ensuring that your favourite independent artist continues to thrive.

In 2001, a work titled 'All That Big Rain Coming From Top Side' by Aboriginal artist Rover Thomas Joolama sold for $778,750, with the National Gallery of Australia securing the piece. Demand for his work spiked after his work appeared in the 1990 Venice Biennale and his exhibition at the National Gallery of Victoria in 1994.

In 2020, Brett Whiteley's 'Henri's Armchair', a painting from his Lavender Bay series, broke an Australian record, landing more than $6 million at auction. Obviously blue-chip artworks aren't the most accessible investment for many people, though. For starters, art doesn't provide any regular income, every artwork has its own specific risk profile, and it's generally considered an illiquid investment – meaning you can't necessarily sell it fast if you need the cash.

That said, there are new opportunities for people who want to invest at a feasible entry price, such as ARTCELS, a service developed by commodities trader Gijs de Viet and London-based contemporary art gallerist Elio D'Anna of the House of Fine Art (HOFA). The pair had a vision to open up contemporary art investment to a young, international market. Their plan was to provide access to shares in a portfolio of works by the likes of Banksy, KAWS, Jeff Koons, Damien Hirst, Takashi Murakami and more. The first opportunity came in 2020, delivered through a virtual exhibition called *XXI*. Viewers could see the collection and make a sole acquisition or opt for a small share of ownership in the portfolio, paying a minimum of £370. The offering of 1000 shares had a complete uptake.

'The value of the works is divided by a number of shares issued and the subscriber can buy these shares, then once the piece is sold, the profits are distributed across the shareholders,' Elio explains.

ARTCELS works to give its investors the best possible opportunity to achieve a return by selecting works that they anticipate will have an appreciative value that will grow in time.

'As an investor, the main benefit of owning shares in the portfolio is that you have the opportunity to benefit from the appreciation of some of the most sought-after works of art that not just anyone could have access to,' Elio says.

While, of course, investors don't get the pleasure of hanging the art around their home, they do get access to private events and exhibitions. In 2020, these were held virtually. Most investors chose to spend between $2000 and $10,000, which Elio says is very appealing because 'if you are looking for investment grade artwork, you would usually need at least $20,000 minimum'.

But what are the benefits of entering the art world in this way – do I simply get to say I own a small part of a Banksy, or is there more to it? Elio explains that, like other investments, I will own equity in the portfolio in the form of shares, which I can trade. 'You have access to an app where you will receive quarterly reports that will allow you to see how your stock is performing.

'Despite the global pandemic, the art market has been steady with some artists and portfolios actually peaking. Banksy, for example, has seen a huge increase in the price of his works, with most important artists following a similar trend,' Elio adds. In recent years, though, there was also a decrease in interest in artists who weren't as well established. The growth in the value of prominent works was attributed to people wanting to diversify as traditional investments such as property and shares became uncertain during the pandemic. 'The surge in acquisitions and record sales in auction results around the world has made the art market favourable to invest in,' Elio says.

By the first quarter of 2021, ARTCELS enhanced its digital platform, enabling shareholders to sell their shares via the app. They also launched the ARTEM token – 'A utility token that converts the shares digitally through the blockchain. You'll be able to have a token that represents your share value so you can exchange that, allowing you to create liquidity for the shares.'

If you're interested in getting into art investment through ART-CELS, you need to register on their website and complete forms and provide security information. Once you have been approved, you'll receive compliance documentation and complete your payment, after which your share certificate will be issued.

While art has been one of the best performing asset classes in the past 100 years, and this is predicted to continue, returns are never a sure thing. But Elio argues, 'I think it's safe to say that very selective and well curated portfolios that have been put together by knowledgeable people within the art market will always maintain their value. But it is important to highlight that there are always going to be risks associated with any type of investment.'

I missed out on the first opportunity, but I add ARTCELS to my list of possible future investment opportunities. I don't need, nor can I afford, a Tesla. But investing in contemporary artists is something that I definitely want to get behind. Not only am I a big fan of investing in the arts, but I also wouldn't mind being able to say I'm the part-owner of some outrageous contemporary piece.

But first I have to find my new home.

Ethical admin checklist

 Speculative investments are just that: speculative. There may be high rewards, but they could also be high-risk.

 New industries are changing rapidly. There might be a speculative investment that's seriously hyped, but it could just as easily be superseded by a disruptor, and fast.

 Not all speculative investments will align with your values. Like any investment, you'll need to check if the business concept and its model aligns with your ethical strategy.

11

Ethical Property Investment

AT THIS POINT, I'VE MADE the decision to move to regional Victoria, but before I commit, I need to decide whether I want to build a sustainable shack from scratch or buy an old property that I can restore and add sustainable retrofits to. I have grand plans to design and build a sustainable property on a block of land, but I quickly realise that building means needing somewhere else to live in the meantime. I also have a strong attraction to heritage homes. Perhaps I could find a property that is kind of raw but has high ceilings and intrinsic value, because there's a limited supply of historic architecture – scarcity is valuable, and there are only so many 100-year-old houses up for grabs, especially within my budget.

One of the biggest problems we face in Australia when it comes to affordable and sustainable housing is the lack of available space. We might complain about monstrous medium- to high-density apartment blocks going up in our leafy suburbs, and yet, as the population grows, we have to create new places to put people. Our ageing population presents an additional challenge. So what's the solution?

Let's first look at the extraordinary amount of unused land we have available to us in this country. It could be better utilised for affordable and sustainable housing. Fortunately, there are businesses popping up to provide a fix.

Planning a sustainable home

Tasmania-based Andrew Kerr runs AKA Architecture, a practice that's focused on sustainable design principles. He practises what he preaches, having built a home that was not only affordable but ethically constructed.

Andrew was no stranger to the land, located in the Huon Valley suburb of Flowerpot, when he bought it for $75,000 ten years ago. 'I used to pick cherries at Flowerpot – that's how I bought my first car and saved my deposit,' Andrew recalls. He purchased the 1.5-hectare site from 'Ted the cherry farmer'. His land is next to the old cherry orchard, which was an apple orchard before that. Today, it's a vineyard.

The original plan was for Andrew's parents to retire at the site. They couldn't afford it at the time, so Andrew made the purchase. Sadly, Andrew's dad passed away before the house was completed. Today, his mum is living in the property after selling the family home. Re-entering the market proved difficult, so part of Andrew's ethical approach to the use of this land has inevitably become finding a way to support our rising need for intergenerational living.

Andrew sought to respect the area's fruit-growing past in his design and aimed to build a home for just $60,000. As part of the build, bushfire risk mitigation was imperative. But instead of chopping down trees and discarding them, Andrew took the timber, which was milled onsite, and turned the short and sometimes imperfect pieces into the timber cladding for the home – creating an apple-crate aesthetic.

Andrew points out that part of a commitment to sustainability involves building a home that doesn't have an obnoxious environmental footprint. You can add a stack of sustainable elements to any home, but if it's freaking massive, you undo all of those considerations. That's why Andrew's home is a humble 61 square metres. It has been designed in line with sustainable practices, which include passive solar design, recycled materials – including an internal wall made of second-hand bricks – and a selection of used roof tiles in a range of colours. 'It's really simple stuff, but it's not yet common practice,' Andrew says.

In addition, he has used salvaged windows, getting four double-glazed pieces free and negotiating to pay only for the aluminium frames. 'There are loads of windows that are either mistakenly ordered (size, colour, double-ups, etc.) or are slightly damaged, taking up warehouse space,' he explains. In this instance, he worked backwards from an architectural perspective, allowing the materials to inform the design. 'The windows were nearly 1200 millimetres wide – about the size of an apple crate – this worked nicely with the short lengths of timber milled from onsite,' he says.

Using recycled goods doesn't mean forgoing style. 'There's a contrast between the rough and the refined,' Andrew says. Indeed, the Apple Crate Shack sits respectfully within its surrounds, while also being incredibly warm and inviting. In the end, the build cost Andrew approximately $103,000. You'd think building something affordable would be a breeze from a financial perspective but, actually, the bank has other ideas. 'Banks want three- or four-bedroom homes. If they have a larger asset, that's easier to sell,' he explains.

It's true – traditionally, the view has been that anything under 60 to 70 square metres is a liability. But that's an outdated way of thinking. Household sizes are decreasing as property prices are rising. Fewer people need, or can afford, a four-bedroom home, but the criteria for mortgage approvals has not moved with the times. Andrew was an emerging architect who'd just opened a practice, and he didn't want the stress or the responsibility of a large mortgage. Nor did he need to whack a behemoth residence on his land.

The straw that broke the camel's back

Dutch-born Joost Bakker, who's now very much a Melburnian, has been described as 'the poster boy for zero-waste'. He's been thinking about how our homes can help us sustain our lives since he was a teenager. 'It started when I was about twelve – I was wondering why we weren't using our buildings to grow food, because that's where we generate lots of nutrients and water,' he recalls.

It might seem like an odd thing for a growing lad to be pondering but, at the time, his family was building a shed on their farm and they designed it so the roof could be used. These early musings would go on to become the centre of Joost's career ethos. In his early years as a florist, he began to experiment with using recycled and upcycled materials in his installations. This paved the way for much larger sustainable projects, including a straw-bale house built in 2006. 'It was the first straw-bale house to make the cover of *Vogue Living*,' Joost says.

He completed a bushfire-proof home in Victoria's Kinglake for restaurateur Dan Zeidan, who lost his home in the Black Saturday bushfires in 2009. Joost designed the home using recycled materials, straw bale, fireproof magnesium oxide board and crushed brick. It was a formula that the CSIRO tested in 2012, taking a structure comprised of the same materials and setting it alight. Flames climbed the walls, but once they were extinguished, the home stood almost exactly as it had prior to the fire, with little more than a few dark marks around the edges.

The Kinglake property was constructed for $605,000, but Joost says variations of this home can be done at a more affordable scale if they're smaller. This particular property has Miele appliances and other optional features. 'It's the footprint that makes it expensive. The bigger you go, the more you use,' he explains.

At his own home, in Melbourne's outer-eastern suburb of Monbulk, Joost has enough land for a vegetable patch and doesn't need to grow his produce on the roof, but he does have a toilet system in which the waste is consumed by worms, which in turn gives him a healthy 'closed loop' system for food growth. Inspired by the results, he turned his hand to designing 'a building that was zero-waste and had a system for utilising the nutrients that were generated'.

Straw and soil remain at the heart of everything Joost is doing because he's staunchly opposed to Forest Stewardship Council (FSC) certified timber. 'It's the ultimate greenwash,' he argues. That's because in many cases it's done nothing to reduce incidents of logging. Land is cleared for trees to be planted in close proximity, and they're sprayed liberally with pesticide, which deters the growth of anything else. 'There's no wildlife, you don't hear birds. I refuse to participate in it,' Joost says. One of the key companies Joost works with is Ortech Industries. They've been making compressed strawboard panels in the Victorian town of Bendigo since 1963.

I want to see these magical fireproof straw panels for myself, so I jump in the car and head to Ortech's manufacturing site. I meet managing director Derek Layfield, who, after starting as a cadet in the business at twenty-three, went on to buy the business, making it what it is today.

'If you get one piece of straw it will burn. If you put it in a panel it carbonises and resists penetration of fire,' Derek explains. 'It's so densely compressed it's like trying to burn a phone book. There's no oxygen to support combustion. It will burn really slowly.

'Straw comes from within 100 kilometres from here, from local farmers. We're taking bulk material and compressing it,' he explains.

We watch the loose straw travel on a conveyor belt into the compression section. He lets me put my hand in and toss the straw around. I can see that it really is just straw, nothing else. Once it's compressed into a panel, it's finished in a recycled paper case that can then be covered with a variety of materials, including textured paint, Colorbond, perforated foil and more.

Next, Derek shows me the fireproofing results in action. A flame-thrower, heated to 3500 degrees Celsius, is lit and placed in direct contact with a straw panel. Remarkably, the panel turns black, but that's about it. There's no smoke because the straw is non-toxic and it's densely packed in the panel. After a few minutes, Derek puts his hand on the back of the panel to highlight the fact that the heat hasn't reached the other side. 'It has protection from radiant heat,' he says. Then a hole is drilled in the panel, and they let me put my finger in it. It's perfectly cool. While the outside of the panel is burnt, the overall damage is minimal.

Building for a changing climate

When Michael Mann, Pennsylvania State University's professor of atmospheric science, visited Australia in January 2020 in the midst of the bushfires, he told *Bloomberg*, 'We're seeing the beginning stages of monumental, catastrophic climate changes that will ultimately drive people away from large inhabited regions of this continent.' He suggested that in the future large chunks of the country could become too hot for human habitation. The result, some suggest, will be increasing environmental migration, in which people will move to more temperate locations. The worst-case scenario is that we'll see a rise in 'climate change refugees' who lose their homes to unliveable conditions.

Consider this: if you're investing in property within the next decade, will the place you choose to live be viable when it comes time to sell in later decades? This might seem like an extreme question, and perhaps it is. But increasingly, the climate in your state could have a very real impact on your property value. It's all well and good to get a dirt-cheap block of bushland and put a sustainable home on it, but could it become worthless if no future communities want to live there?

Dr Ian Weir suggests we can build for climate change rather than fearing it. He was raised in a southern West Australian farming district and is an architect and academic at Queensland University of Technology. 'We know how to make a building withstand more destructive fires than bushfires, but we aren't yet applying those principles more broadly,' he says. The common perception is that bushfire-proof housing is expensive and materials aren't sustainable, but that's not the case.

If you're considering buying regional land, your first task is to understand the Bushfire Attack Level (BAL) rating. A BAL rating is based on the likely exposure to ember attack, flames and radiant heat. The rating sets the requirements for your build. For any home with a BAL rating, Dr Weir says the first principle is to use non-combustible materials including metal, cement-based products and masonry. After the bushfires of 2019–20, Dr Weir predicts that architects will increasingly work with fire engineers to build more innovative solutions rather than 'the lazy tick-the-box approach that the profession has used to date'.

'I get many enquiries from people trying to decide whether or not to buy a high-fire-risk property and I remind them that it is an immense privilege to be able to dwell within such bushland biodiverse sites in Australia,' Dr Weir says.

'Where else in the world can you have such exclusion, privacy and connectivity with natural systems that are so biodiverse?' he adds, and suggests that far from being a poor investment, well-designed bushfire-proof homes will be increasingly sought after.

'We have huge scope for real innovation if we treat bushfire as a catalyst for creativity,' he concludes.

Building is one thing, but insurance is another. In 2019, the Climate Council issued a report indicating Australia's changing climate could result in property value losses of $571 billion by 2030, $611 billion by 2050, and $770 billion by 2100. Oh, and if you buy in a risky area, there's every chance insurers will decline to provide you with the necessary protection.

According to the report, one in nineteen property owners could experience insurance premiums that are unaffordable by 2030. The document also suggests that at particular risk are low-lying properties near rivers and coastlines, with rising sea levels and erosion becoming an increasingly significant threat by 2050. This is certain to reduce the appeal of buying a coveted beach house in a flashy location.

Will Steffen, Australian National University professor and member of the Climate Council, suggests the impact of climate change in the next decade is already locked in as a result of past emissions. 'If you look at 2030, there's a lot we can say with a high degree of confidence,' he says. Front of mind is bushfire risk. 'That's going to be worse in 2030 than it is now. If you have properties in fire-prone areas that didn't burn this year, insurance companies will look at those areas,' he explains.

That's because areas that have recently burnt will take time to regenerate and therefore have some years of protection ahead until the fuel load rises once again. For those looking to buy a home, he says, 'You wouldn't go to areas with high bushfire risk and you wouldn't go to the coast.' He says that's because at the current rate of change, sea levels are expected to rise 40 to 80 centimetres in the coming decades. 'If we don't get our emissions down, we can expect rises of up to 80 centimetres and getting close to a metre in the next 100 years,' Professor Steffen warns.

Risking it all for the dream home

The city of Shoalhaven, on the New South Wales South Coast, is dotted with idyllic coastal towns. Residents have the best of both worlds: crystal-clear ocean on their doorstep and massive national parks beyond the back fence. It's little wonder good properties can easily fetch $1 million or more in some parts. Who wouldn't want to live here? Well, one serious risk is bushfire.

Anouk and her husband, Steele, found their dream slice of land in 2011: a 29-hectare stretch of perfection with its own creek and a state forest on the boundary line. Back then it only had a rundown '80s-style shack and a shed on it, but the potential to build a sustainable home to suit a family lifestyle with their kids was huge. In the years after they bought, the couple fixed up the shack to make it liveable, added additional container-style accommodation and lived off-grid, while working with council to establish their options. There was the work with a bushfire consultant to recommend the asset protection zone (APZ), to determine the BAL rating. 'Our rating ended up being BAL 19 – the higher the rating, the tougher the fireproofing building standards are, which increases the cost of the build. For example, at BAL 19 you can have hardwood timber window frames but above this they must be metal,' Anouk explains.

They experienced several knockbacks and challenges as they attempted to bring their dream home to life. But before they could, the 2019 bushfires took out the shack, the container and a shed full of materials Steele had been collecting for their sustainable build. As they'd been living like this 'temporarily', they had no insurance and subsequently lost everything but a few car and trailer loads of possessions and the earth under their feet. Needless to say, it was not a happy new year. Fortunately, the family got out safely well in advance and had accommodation with friends nearby. A few months later, they were able to buy a small termite-infested shack. Steele, a carpenter, tore through a reno at lightning pace and the investment property became the family home. In the meantime, the state-funded fire damage clean-up was completed in June 2020, six months after the event.

'We are really privileged, we kept our jobs,' Anouk, who works in health, admits, and says many are much worse off. Tourism businesses folded and several locals remain in unstable accommodation. Which is perhaps why she has a bright outlook. 'Did you know you can make cakes in a barbecue?' she laughs.

Anouk says they've learnt so much from their experience, and this will inform their decisions as they redesign and resubmit their application. How long will it take for them to get a house on the land?

'Maybe six years?' Anouk wonders.

To those considering a similar path, Anouk suggests: 'Understand your rural zoning. Can the land be used for agriculture or ecotourism? If you intend to live there, you have to make sure you have a dwelling entitlement. And of course, think about your fire risk.'

Risk due diligence

I found a property listed in a bushfire-prone location and I was seriously considering it. Before I made an offer, I looked into home and contents insurance premiums.

It's possible to opt for home insurance only (the building), contents insurance only (all the stuff you own), or both. If you're a buyer, you might need to insure a specific amount as part of your home loan requirements. I want both home and contents covered. It will cover me in the event of bushfire, flood or other forms of unexpected damage. Of course, if a bushfire rips through this weatherboard home I'm considering, it would be flattened, so I would be insuring to build something new, plus replace all of my belongings.

Factors that might impact the cost of your premium include:

- The type of cover (home, contents or both)

- The amount you want to insure the property for (what it's worth)

- Your excess (the amount you're charged if you make a claim)

- Your previous history of insurance claims

- The location of the home and the prevalence of natural disaster or crime

- The materials your home is constructed from and any additional special features.

According to 2021 research by Canstar, insurance premium averages, based on home insurance of between $300,000 and $1.2 million and contents cover of $50,000, varies from state to state. For example, in New South Wales the average is $1401 for home insurance and $431 for contents. That's $1424 per year. In South Australia, it's $990 for home and $349 for contents insurance. But up in Far North Queensland, it's a whopping $4296 for home insurance and $891 for contents, or a hefty $4813 per year as a package. That price is in line with the prevalence of natural disasters in the area.

In Melbourne, where I'm from, I'm up for $1177 for home insurance and $377 for my contents if I buy in the city. But when I apply for a quote on a property in a bushfire-prone regional town, my anticipated home and contents premium on a weatherboard property is around $3000 a year, and I've based this on a rebuild of a conservative $400,000. This is a serious consideration, as it's an extra $250 a month I'd need to fork out on top of my mortgage. Not to mention bills, rates, petrol and, you know, living.

Five days after the house was listed, it sold for well over my budget, so the problem was quickly resolved. But it did make me think twice about what I could afford. If you're going bush, those insurance premiums are going to sting. Something for me to keep in mind as my search continues.

A southern breeze

In January 2020, Tasmania's new premier, Peter Gutwein, became the state's first Liberal minister for climate change, expressing a strong commitment to be a leader on the issue. The state has seen solid growth in recent years, drawing people in huge numbers thanks in part to the impressive tourism offering, particularly the Museum of Old and New Art (MONA), wineries and natural wonders.

Dr Lisa Denny, research fellow at the Institute for Social Change at the University of Tasmania, echoes the sentiments of Professor Steffen, saying that early research conducted by the institute does show anecdotal evidence of people being drawn to Tasmania for a combination of lifestyle factors, including the implications of climate change.

In 2019, Dr Denny released a discussion paper called 'Moving to Tassie' – a brief examination of internal migration to Tasmania co-authored by colleagues Nick Osbaldiston and Felicity Picken. The paper is part of a research project exploring the specific motivations of people leaving other states for the island. The survey data shows a number of reasons that new residents are setting up down south, including climate, environment, safety, work-life balance and community.

'Our research has shown that the decision-making process about where people live is changing and we know that climate and the environment is one of the prevailing factors,' Dr Denny says.

'We hypothesised that they were moving due to lack of opportunities, but climate is impacting people even more so. People are starting to make decisions based on their ability to insure their homes too,' she adds.

According to their paper, one of the biggest groups entering Tasmania from 2012 to 2019 were those between the ages of twenty-five and twenty-nine. Plus, a significant number of small children have entered the state, in line with the migration of their parents – a group aged between twenty-five and forty-four. That said, a sudden swell in interstate migrants is always going to create new challenges. According to Dr Denny, more than 80 per cent of Tasmania's population growth is migration-driven. 'That puts pressure on our infrastructure and amenities,' she says. But it's not happening evenly across the map. 'We've got a two-speed economy. The south of the state has experienced extreme population pressures; the northwest is struggling to keep its population, Dr Denny explains.

In areas where migration-driven growth has been rapid, housing development needs have been intense. And yet there is a skills shortage in the construction sector, traffic congestion is worsening and long-term residents are unhappy. So anything that's idyllic and broadly appealing inevitably becomes increasingly unattractive if large swathes of the population try to do the same thing simultaneously.

Katrina and Nick Carr moved from Melbourne to Hobart in 2016. The pair met in Melbourne, where Katrina's from, while Nick was working as a clinical perfusionist at the Alfred Hospital, but a move to Hobart was on the cards as Nick was originally from Tassie. The couple had two small children so a suitable living environment for their growing family was a priority.

After living in Hobart for twelve months, they bought a threebedroom house in the suburb of Rose Bay in 2017 for $380,000. It was the perfect entry into the market, and well-timed too. They sold the house eighteen months later for approximately $200,000 more than they paid for it. They've since bought a larger family home in Lindisfarne for $725,000.

'While the market is definitely strong here, you could still buy a three- or four-bedroom house within twenty to twenty-five minutes of the city for less than $600,000,' Katrina says, but adds, 'Everything definitely sells very quickly here, and with no auctions you need to be fast with your offers.'

The climate was definitely a drawcard. Although it gets cold in winter, there's not too much rain, so winter days are often cold but sunny. 'We do get snow in winter, which is beautiful; it's pretty special to walk through the city and see snow on the mountain. I am also very fortunate to see it from my lounge room too,' Katrina says.

But the best part is the traffic, or lack of it. 'My commute is about ten to fifteen minutes. Compared to living in Melbourne, I've gained two hours back in my day. Life is definitely easier here – the commute and stress of running around is just not there.' There's less choice in schools, she points out, but she's still happy with where the kids are enrolled. Inevitably, though, the many attractive lifestyle and economic drivers have made Hobart a more popular place to live. 'Houses in my area are selling to cash buyers in a matter of days. I can only assume the cash buyers are coming from interstate,' Katrina says.

Ethical admin checklist

 Buy or build? Both have their pros and cons from an ethical standpoint. You might be able to get a really affordable bush block, but you need to do your due diligence.

 Consider long-term liveability. It might be okay for now, but will your chosen location still be desirable in years to come? The impact of climate change in certain regions may affect your property value and insurance rates in the future.

 If you're considering a sustainable build, you'll need to spend time thinking about the materials you want to use and how the build will come together. Research suppliers and sources of recyclable materials before starting.

12

Sustainability Retrofits

WE'VE EXPLORED SOME OPTIONS FOR sustainable building materials, but what else can you do to make sustainable improvements to your home that don't cost a fortune? There are a few things you can do without a huge outlay that could make a big difference to the running cost of your home and its long-term value.

Harnessing the sun

There's never been a better time to install solar, with many states offering rebates as incentives for people who switch to renewable energy. The cost of installing solar will vary depending on where you're located and how much power you desire. Generally speaking, a small 1.5 kilowatt system could cost you approximately $3000, while a 10 kilowatt system might set you back $10,000.

For a standard household, a 6.6 kilowatt system is generally deemed suitable, but smaller systems can still have their benefits. There may also be considerable incentives depending on where your home is. In August 2018, the Victorian government launched its Solar

Homes Program as part of a push to get residents to install solar, offering a $1850 rebate. Even if you're not eligible for a rebate, installing solar can pay dividends quickly. The immediate benefits are environmental. Replacing fossil-fuel generated power with solar ensures that you're using a renewable energy source that doesn't contribute to greenhouse gas emissions.

In addition, you're likely to receive 'feed-in tariffs'. That means you get paid for generating energy that you return to the grid. So, if you're not home and your house is producing excess electricity, it can be sold back into the grid at a feed-in tariff rate. These rates vary from state to state and depend on the size of your solar offering. It's worth checking that your energy provider is offering a competitive rate: some pay as low as 7 cents per kilowatt, while you might get 20 cents or more in some parts of the country.

This is not something you can do without expert input. You'll need a Clean Energy Council professional to do the installation if you want to be eligible for a rebate. They can also take out a lot of the hassle, managing the purchase of the system components along with the installation. They'll also guide the placement of the panels, to ensure you get the best possible energy outcome, without it encroaching on the aesthetic appeal of your home. Generally, north-facing solar panels will deliver great results, but east- or west-facing panels can still capture morning or afternoon light.

If you're building from scratch, it may pay to engage an architect. Antony Martin, director of MRTN Architects, is thinking well beyond the present day when he factors solar into the design of his homes. Take, for example, Nulla Vale, in Victoria, a project which is completely off-grid. The client had funds for a small, 50-square-metre home, but they plan to build an additional three-bedroom residence on the site in time. With this in mind, they pimped out their small property with enough solar panels to power the home they'll build later. This meant designing the small dwelling to accommodate the panels, and even making them a design feature. 'The client realised they had to pay for the systems for the house now. We built simply so that we could afford to put in the systems,' Antony explains.

From the beginning of the project, that meant considering the orientation of the building as well as the pitch of the roof. 'With your typical photovoltaic panel array, the roof pitch is about 23 degrees to get the best collection,' he says. But Antony points out that in Victoria there's less sun exposure than in other parts of Australia, so they took the roof pitch to 45 degrees to optimise the effectiveness of the panels and increase the potential for battery storage.

Designing for a sustainable future has become the norm for Antony and his team. They consider everything from induction cooktops to electric cars. 'In the systems we're proposing there's a greater reliance on electricity. These features might not go in straightaway, but we're always planning for it,' he says. 'We're now suggesting that clients don't need a gas connection,' Antony adds. That means even if his clients don't have the funds for things such as solar or heat pump technology for hydronic heating, new builds and renovations are always completed in a manner that allows homeowners to add these elements over time. 'The photovoltaic panel location and orientation is always considered – it's the norm, not the exception,' Antony says.

Battery power

For all the areas where Australia falls down on renewable investment, we're increasingly leading the charge when it comes to batteries. Until recently, Australia was home to the world's biggest lithium-ion battery, known as the Tesla big battery, located at the Hornsdale Power Reserve in South Australia. At the time its capacity was 100 megawatts / 129 megawatt hour and was upgraded to 150 megawatts / 194 megawatt hour, but it has since been outdone by the Gateway project in the East Otay Mesa community in San Diego, California, which has a capacity of 250 megawatts.

We have plenty of reasons to be optimistic about our future potential, though. In 2020, the ACT government was looking into installing a battery for the new suburb of Jacka. The residents of up to 500 homes would have access to battery and solar power.

In November 2020, the Andrews Labor government announced plans for the Victorian Big Battery, a 300-megawatt battery to be located near the Moorabool Terminal Station, just out of Geelong. Operations began in 2021 but, unfortunately, it caught fire that August. It's understood to be the first battery mega pack fire in the world. Let's hope it was an isolated incident.

For those who don't have access to community battery power, is it still too prohibitive to make the switch? The truth is it can take years to get a return on your investment, with the cost of battery and installation still too high for the average Aussie. The Tesla Powerwall launched in Australia back in 2015. Version 2.0 was released in 2020 and offered double the capacity of the first edition, but its price also spiked from approximately $9600 to $11,700, plus installation.

In some states there are incentive schemes that will reduce your 'payback time'. That's the time it takes for the investment costs to be covered through reduced power bills and income derived from feed-in tariffs. Subsidies, coupled with savings on bills, could reduce your payback time to about five or six years, but if you're not eligible for incentives, that could be much longer.

Your cost of living may determine your capacity to make such a significant investment. I met Rachel and Karl Russo from the Victorian town of Loch a few years ago. They'd found an abandoned house that no one else wanted; they bought it for $30,000 and moved it to their land (the transportation cost was another $30,000). They've since done extensive restoration work and are now doing what they can to make it as sustainable as possible. The extraordinarily low cost of their dwelling, and the fact that they've renovated much of the home themselves, has freed up the funds required to add some serious bells and whistles.

'For us the choice of Tesla Powerwalls was both aesthetic and practical. They are so compact, and we don't have a lot of space in the garage where they are fitted. The alternative option would have taken up at least four times the space,' Karl tells me. He admits it was a significant investment, but absolutely necessary to support their off-grid lifestyle. Karl and Rachel invested a hefty $60,000 in battery and solar resources: this includes two Powerwalls and a solar farm in their paddock, as well as specialist installation by Melbourne-based BREC. They were eligible for the small-scale technology certificate (STC), which allowed them to get a rebate of about $5400.

'It's a big chunk of our budget, but it was an easy decision for us,' Karl says. 'We have a very remote property with no power connection and our driveway is nearly 2 kilometres long, so you can imagine how much it would have cost to run mains power up to the house.'

While Karl admits it was 'bloody expensive', the couple put money away over the course of the restoration with the aim of buying the batteries at the end, in the hope that the technology would get better while they waited, and it did. 'I do see it as a valuable investment – it feels amazing to be running off the sun. It's so satisfying to check the app to see how much power is feeding in at any time of the day. It also makes us aware of our consumption,' Karl explains.

But being off-grid, they're not eligible for feed-in tariffs, so while they have no power bills, they can't gain financially. That means it will take longer than average for the investment to pay for itself – 'maybe ten to twelve years', Karl predicts. 'But for us, it's more of a necessity, so we're not too hung up on that.'

When we speak, it's early summer and the batteries have just been installed. Karl says there have been no problems or disadvantages to running off batteries but anticipates challenges in winter. 'We'll be installing a back-up generator before then, which will kick in automatically and charge the Powerwalls if they ever get too low,' he says.

Karl and Rachel haven't stopped at battery power when it comes to sustainability – they've gone all out, treating their waste with a worm farm composting system, catching their own water and planting 75,000 native trees with the support of Landcare, so they'll have a regenerative firewood supply. 'So the property will be carbon negative – woo!' Karl concludes enthusiastically.

Pre-loved interior styling

The alternative to building a sustainable home is of course to buy something existing and retro-fit it. If you're creative, you can do this on a shoestring. Take Tim Gauci and his partner, Nicole Langelier. After buying a rundown cottage in Hepburn Springs – Victoria's spa country – they set themselves a challenge to refurbish it using as many recycled and repurposed materials as possible.

After purchasing the rundown shell in January 2019, their little getaway, La Villetta, is now complete. 'Most of the fixtures and fittings are recycled: island bench, range, fridge, tiles in the wet room, kitchen and ensuite,' Tim says. Even the internal doors were salvaged from the local tip. In addition, most of the structural timber is recycled. 'It came up exactly as we had hoped. Rustic. Perfectly imperfect,' he says.

According to Tim, the key to renovating with pre-loved materials is not to have a specific plan. 'Rather, find key pieces that are in line with the look you are going for,' he says. It's the flexibility that enables you to save. For example, the couple managed to score a $4800 benchtop with sink for just $350, so they made the island bench to suit it. But where do you get such a find? Tim says Facebook Marketplace, Gumtree and hard-rubbish collections are the places to get an absolute steal. He explains that heaps of people buy things then decide they don't suit and advertise on social media to offload the unwanted wares.

That includes a stack of things you might not expect: tapware, vanities, sinks, bathtubs, ex-floor stock, toilets, lighting, doors and even whole sets of kitchen cabinetry are up for grabs if you're prepared to scour sites. The biggest saving is often found in large pieces of discarded timber. 'Solid timber can be sanded and sprayed – instant Hamptons-style kitchens, light fittings, window furnishings and flooring,' Tim points out. If you're not a professional builder, Tim says it's a good idea to ask your tradie if the items you've found will fit, and ensure they are useable.

With the budget renovation completed, the value of their property has improved by 35 per cent. The pair plan to keep it as a weekender and will occasionally put it on Airbnb for approximately $400 per night. They've worked out that leasing it for just forty-five nights per year will cover their costs. There's nothing second-rate about that.

Rooftop greenification and permaculture

If you live in the city or have limited land, the prospect of putting a garden on the roof could be very appealing, for the natural beauty, the reduction in home running costs, and the value-add it provides.

Sara Wilkinson is professor of sustainable property at the University of Technology Sydney and has spent several years investigating the impact of rooftop greenification in Australia and around the world. According to Sara, 32 per cent of horizontal surfaces in Sydney are rooftops, and the potential for greenification is largely untapped. Sara believes that in Australia we could benefit from a 'carrot and stick' approach, meaning there could be a combination of incentives to install 'green' roofs and legislation that sets out new expectations.

She points to the city of Toronto, which has a mandated approach. Toronto was the first North American city to adopt a green roof bylaw, back in 2009. It requires all new developments greater than 2000 square metres in gross floor area to greenify 20 to 60 per cent of the roof space. The program is considered a success, with approximately 420 green roof permits issued for the development of 450,000 square metres of roof space.

By contrast, Singapore has set up a voluntary program, and it has resulted in the biggest uptake of green roofs in the world. 'There are cultural differences to take into account and so a voluntary approach in another country might not produce the same results,' Sara points out. But the results are encouraging, nonetheless.

In 2018, Sara and her colleagues completed a study, 'Expanding the Living Architecture in Australia', in which they explored how Australian cities could adopt a green roofs and green walls (GRGW) program. They compared five cities with existing mandatory or voluntary green roof measures in place: Toronto, Singapore, London, Rotterdam and Stockholm.

'We took the results from each city and then looked at all the development applications in Sydney and Melbourne CBDs and worked out the number of green roofs that would have been delivered following each program,' she explains.

The report shows Singapore is marketing itself as a garden city to attract investment, tourism and economic growth. 'This approach resulted in an 805% increase in GRGW and a flourishing GRGW economy,' the report reads.

There are benefits for owners, the community and the economy, with owners seeing a property value uplift, a reduction in energy consumption and even the potential for a reduced insurance premium. The community benefits from improved air quality, reduced impact on stormwater and improved biodiversity. Finally, the installation of green roofs creates jobs in design, installation and maintenance, boosting economic activity.

Importantly, from a private investment perspective, Sara's research indicates that people who install green roofs are likely to benefit in the long term. 'A good argument is the value-add to real estate – properties with good green infrastructure tend to attract a premium in sale and rental prices, and have lower vacancy rates,' she says.

That's not to say it's easy. There are many factors to consider. 'On a new build house, you'll be looking at ensuring the roof structure can bear the dead and live loads of the green roof,' she says. Additional requirements include provision of a waterproof membrane, planting and irrigation. But, she adds, 'you will get energy savings through improved thermal insulation, and so heating and cooling operating costs will be lower'.

People living in apartments have options too. She suggests green walls on balconies. She also recently visited Canberra, where green walls had been installed around car-parking enclosures. In new developments where there is rooftop access, she's also seeing a rise in communal green rooftop spaces.

If you want to have a crack at installing a green roof, you need to consider the same factors that you would for any garden. 'You should select plants that suit the climate. Of course, indigenous plants are a great choice. This is also good because these plants attract pollinators and biodiversity to ensure the plants thrive,' Sara says. It's best to look into what grows well in your state, as local species are used to the weather. 'Although climate change is going to alter that to some degree,' she adds.

You'll also need to treat your roof like you would your backyard. 'Depending on the plant species selected, you may need to weed and replace plants occasionally.' Finally, you'll need to factor in the cost of water and irrigation and any maintenance that might be required.

Sara is optimistic about greenifying our architecture and the impact that it could have. 'There is no reason why we could not be net-positive in terms of green infrastructure in our cities. By that I mean if the City of Sydney CBD local government area is 2.8 square kilometres, then our green roofs and walls could exceed that total. How good would it be to put back more than was there when humans started to settle the area?'

But it's more than just a pleasant goal to strive towards – it's becoming a design imperative as average temperatures rise and it becomes dangerous, if not impossible, for people to work outside. Sara predicts this may impact productivity in construction and other sectors.

'We know that good levels of green infrastructure attenuates the urban heat island. We need to plan and act now for our future. Our cities will become less attractive to live, work and invest in if we don't,' she concludes.

Even if you don't go all out with a green roof, simple permaculture considerations can provide a sustainability boost, particularly if you grow your own fruit and vegetables. Permaculture is a design principle based on developing sustainable environments that work in harmony with nature and the local ecology. Whether you have a balcony or a farm, you can practise the philosophy and grow produce that naturally thrives in your home's climate. That means researching what grows well in your region at any given time of year.

With a very small investment, you might be able to grow fruit and vegetables that reduce the cost of your grocery bill. If you have a bigger piece of land, you might also go large-scale, and produce enough fresh food to sell at local farmers' markets, boosting your income.

Cost of permits, planning and approval

If you are considering sustainability retrofits for an existing home, you'll need to check if there are any permits or approvals required before you complete the work, so that you can factor this into your budget. The costs and requirements vary from state to state, but building permits will be needed on most projects, even if they're small.

In addition to permits – the cost of which will vary depending on the extent of the works – you'll also want to make sure your builder is registered with the local building practitioners board. They'll also need to provide insurance information if the cost of the work exceeds a certain amount.

To give you an idea of what you might be up for, a permit for works of around $50,000 might cost a few hundred dollars, but a new building could cost you about $2000 in permit fees.

Retrofit impact

Whether you're building a new home or completing a serious retrofit, it's now likely that you'll need to meet the National Construction Code's minimum building energy efficiency requirements. The best way to do that is through the Nationwide House Energy Rating Scheme (NatHERS). It could be a good idea to do this before you start works, as the NatHERS assessor will check your potential energy rating and also provide advice before you get started. NatHERS provides a star rating out of ten.

In the short term, a house with more than seven stars is likely to have significantly reduced bills due to low power consumption. But it can also be beneficial when you sell, according to research from the Sustainable Buildings Research Centre at the University of Wollongong, as homes with a strong energy efficiency rating can attract a premium compared to dwellings with a lower result.

However, this is still hard to measure with any certainty because the ACT is currently the only place that has made the disclosure of energy efficiency ratings mandatory for sellers. But as the cost of bills continues to rise, this will be an increasingly important consideration for homebuyers, so it could be wise to get on the front foot now.

If you're planning to buy an existing home with sustainability features, finance providers are increasingly offering incentives to do so. Bank Australia offers a Clean Energy Home Loan, which provides discounted rates for people who buy a home with a NatHERS rating of seven stars or more.

Ethical admin checklist

 Which sustainability retrofits are best? That will depend on your home and your budget. Solar could be a great option, but you'll need the agreement of other owners if you're in an apartment, for example. Batteries are still quite expensive too, so you need to consider how long it will be before you get a return on that investment in the form of reduced bills.

 Retrofits don't have to be expensive. Greenification, vegetable gardens and upcycling can be a great start.

 Major works will require planning and permits. It's wise to talk to your local council before getting started.

13

The Future of
Ethical Investing

YOU CAN *NEVER* PREDICT THE FUTURE. I mean, did you anticipate being locked in your house for long stretches of 2020 and 2021? I sure as hell didn't. What we do know is that we've ended up with plenty of time to sit around and think as a result of Covid-19. What's truly important to us? For many, that's increased financial security. But getting rich isn't necessarily the goal – it's simpler than that. In my case, it's building buffer funds to protect myself in the event of another catastrophic global event, but also investing in a way that might enhance both our present and our future.

I'm done taking stuff for granted. After months of on-and-off lockdowns spent with my cats, I find so much joy, even more than before, in simply having coffee with friends, browsing in second-hand furniture stores and going for a long walk beyond a designated radius. A full life doesn't have to cost a massive wedge of your income.

What struck me during the early stages of the lockdowns in 2020, when this was a new experience for everyone on the planet, was that community and connectivity emerged as vital. I mean, I never want to return to Friday nights spent playing trivia on group video calls, but I did find the way we banded together pretty damn heartening.

In researching and writing this book, I've realised there is a huge difference between working towards being 'rich' and developing strategies to achieve positive wealth. The many people I've spoken to have helped me to realise that wealth is a long game, but it delivers dividends over time, not just the big chunk of change you build up, but also in the collective wealth for society that comes with investing wisely. What a privilege it is to have money to invest at all. With this gift, I am determined to put more funds into ventures that will have a meaningful impact. Not just for my generation, but for those who follow.

Our superannuation industry is worth $3 trillion. Imagine what could be done if that was invested with positive social and environmental outcomes in mind. As a collective, we have real power to drive change. Clearly, I'm not alone in this thinking: in June 2021, Bloomberg reported that Australian Ethical's CEO, John McMurdo, indicated that around two years ago, Australians' interest in ethical funds sat at around 15 per cent of the population. Now, interest in ethical investing has spiked, with studies showing that anywhere between 60 and 80 per cent of people are open to it. McMurdo described this as a 'seismic shift'.

Australian Ethical has at least $5.4 billion in funds under management, and that's just a fraction of the total figure currently invested in super and shares in Australia. Given it's been around since 1994, Australian Ethical definitely has street cred. Its main super fund has returned approximately 11 per cent annually since it kicked off. That's compared with between 7 and 8 per cent returns on the ASX.

Personally, my super is still with Verve. I'm happy with my returns and generally happy with the contents of my portfolio. Plus, in mid-2021, Verve announced it was adding a Gender Equality Index to help guide its investment decisions. Through this lens they rank companies on key pillars including gender pay parity, sexual harassment and workplace safety, inclusivity, flexible work, and women in leadership.

An excellent move in my view as, at the time this was announced, no other fund had a filter like this. Kind of stunning really, with women, you know, playing a considerable part in the economy and our future prosperity! Plus, in September 2021, Verve announced that they had new financial backing from some prominent female entrepreneurs, including Carol Schwartz, chair of the Women's Leadership Institute Australia, and Jess and Stef Dadon, founders of vegan shoe company Twoobs.

Women in finance are an emerging force in Australia. You only have to turn to Instagram to see the number of women talking openly about money, investing and retirement funds. Don't take my anecdotal social media searches as gospel, though – serious research backs up my theory.

According to the ASX Investor Study 2020, there's been an influx of 'next generation investors getting into investing'. In the twelve-month reporting period, 45 per cent of those who started investing in the year were women.

'It's a trend that looks set to accelerate, with women accounting for 51 per cent of "intending" investors,' the report reads – meaning more women than men intend to invest in the next twelve months.

Say what you will about millennials and gen Z being lazy, entitled and crap with money – we are inevitably going to take over the world in the next decade or so. Some lucky members of this generation will inherit considerable wealth from the baby boomers, and they generally have a strong sense of social justice. Couple that with their technological dexterity and these two generations are about to become incredibly powerful.

If I was an old-school investment company, pouring customers' money into dying industries, I'd be pretty bloody worried. While climate change rallies have impact, so too does voting with your money.

As people become increasingly aware of how their money is invested, they are proactively moving into things that are better aligned with their values and their hopes for the future. If entire generations stop investing in fossil-fuel-related activities such as mining, shit's going to get real.

I heart ethical living

The only thing I knew for certain in early 2021 was that my resolve to live a simpler life was absolutely firm, and that meant moving to a regional town as soon as possible. I clearly wasn't alone. In May 2021, the Australian Bureau of Statistics reported that 43,000 Australians moved to regional locations in 2020, with Melbourne taking the biggest hit – 26,000 Melburnians pulled the plug on city life. I didn't need the ABS to tell me that – I was going to property inspections with hundreds of other latte-sipping Melburnians who wanted out.

In a March 2021 column for *The Australian*, demographer Bernard-Salt described people like me as Virus Escapees Seeking Provincial Australia (VESPAs), and while that's not quite as catchy as his 'smashed avocado' metaphor, I suspect we'll see the trend continue. With working from home and flexible arrangements remaining in place for many people, and more affordable property prices outside the main cities, it's no wonder people are hitting the road en masse. The benefit, I hope, will be an ongoing invigoration of historic towns and local economies, with the dual impact of reduced carbon footprints for those who can walk to shops and schools.

After searching across Victoria and being priced out of some of the initial locations I had my eye on, I settled on Ballarat. Its heritage homes, proximity to Melbourne, infrastructure, food, wine and arts culture made it an attractive location for me. I believe there is still plenty of growth to be achieved here, as more people like me seek historic towns to live in with easy access to the city. I started driving to Ballarat every weekend. I scheduled inspections at properties that I didn't even like, just so that I could meet the agents and get on their radar.

On a hot February morning in 2021, I inspected a property that I just happened to be driving past on the way to another. I met the agent and told her that this wasn't the property for me, I was looking for a heritage home with a Victorian or Edwardian facade. She took my details and told me she'd be in touch if anything came up. A week later, I received a text message from her husband, an agent for the same real estate agency. He had a property that was soon to be listed and asked if I'd like to come and look at it on the evening that they were planning to take the advertising photos. Seeing the property prior to it officially going to market would put me in a good position.

I looked at the old listing online to decide if it was worth a trip. It was a Victorian residence, built circa 1910. There was old floral carpet in the hallway and living room, black-and-white floor tiles in the kitchen and meals area, lime-green paint on the walls and a disgusting brown bathroom.

I could see the potential, though, and perhaps the current owners had since made improvements. So I hit the road and arrived at dusk to take a peek. An intuitive feeling laced its way through my body as I stepped into the hallway. *This is the one.* Despite the faded floral carpet and the hallway with its blood red and patchy white paint scheme, I just knew. It had magnificent high ceilings, bedrooms with original fireplaces and ornate features throughout. The bathroom had been updated with creamy subway tiles and vintage copper shower heads.

After a brief period of negotiation, it was mine. I'd achieved my goal, and a move was on the horizon.

*

I'm now getting settled into my new home. My house isn't as sustainable as I want it to be. Yet. But I view it as sustainable because I've purchased a historic property and have chosen to restore it to its former glory, rather than being responsible for the carbon emissions that come with building from scratch. In the immediate future, I will complete small fixes myself and upcycle where possible. For example, the floral carpet has been lifted and the floorboards beneath will be sanded and refinished, and I have repurposed the carpet, turning the offcuts into a hallway runner and a rug for the living room. Where possible, I'll also use upcycled fixtures and fittings

While I've never been much of a green thumb, I'm pleased to have a large space that I'm turning into a vegetable patch, so that I can eat fresh produce plucked directly from the garden, and reduce the waste associated with my plastic-wrapped supermarket fruit and veg.

The long-term plan is to make small design changes and retrofits that will make the home more efficient. These include solar panels, double-glazed energy-efficient windows and a fresh coat of light-coloured paint on the exterior, which will reduce the heat the residence holds in summer. In time, I'd like to be in a position to switch over to battery power too.

Honestly, the most unsustainable thing about my home is the way it's currently funded – through a Big Four bank that I don't wish to support long term. Given I was working as a freelancer and contractor, I had to take the loan I could secure in my current financial position. However, in the next year or two, I intend to pay down some of the mortgage and refinance with the bank of my choice. My ultimate aspiration is to move to Bank Australia's Clean Energy home loan. To do this, I need to get my property up to a NatHERS rating of seven stars (or higher). That would make me eligible for a discount on my interest rate too.

Improving my ethical share portfolio

Now that I finally have the property, I'm in a position to put more energy into my shares. As of today, I have more than $2000 invested in my Spaceship Earth and Universe portfolio. For the most part, that's come from auto-investing $40 per week. I have also bought ethical ETFs through Pearler worth $1000. I have an auto-invest function set up, so every time I reach $500, I buy units of BetaShares Global Sustainability Leaders ETF (ETHI) and Battery Tech and Lithium ETF (ACDC), which is focused on renewable energy storage solutions.

However, it's worth pointing out that the production of batteries comes with its own complex web of ethical issues. I can't say that lithium mining is ethical. And yet battery storage and the electric vehicle sector are primed for growth. And there are several companies focused on the recycling and repurposing of it to extend its lifespan. The ETFs include several leading electric vehicle manufacturers, and I broadly support this mode of transportation when compared to petrol and diesel vehicles. On balance, I've decided to put a small share of my funds into ACDC but I'm continuing to watch the ETF space and seek out more ethical alternatives.

I'd also like to start buying individual company shares, both to diversify and ensure I'm 100 per cent invested in companies that I wholeheartedly believe in. As it stands, there is no one managed fund or ETF that is extremely ethical, in my view. That is, some have companies that are questionable in their ethics, but because they don't engage in direct fossil fuel production, they make the cut. I suspect, however, that as the ethical sector grows, we'll see more impressive options in time.

The future is green

When I started researching ethical investment in late 2019, it still felt remarkably niche to me. I didn't know anyone investing ethically, and the information available to new investors was limited at best. Over the course of two years, though, ethical investment has increasingly become a standard consideration, particularly for the millennials and gen Z folks I've spoken to. It's a subject covered regularly in finance podcasts, and I'm seeing it in mainstream media now too.

I can only conclude that as it saturates the zeitgeist, investors' increasing appetite for ethical options will continue to steer a change in investing habits. While I don't have a crystal ball, I am certain there is a perfect storm of economic conditions brewing that will drive exponential growth of this sector in the next ten to twenty years. Here are a couple of reasons why:

Post-pandemic values

Covid-19 has been a blessing and a curse. It's made us realise what's truly valuable: security and a safe, happy environment for future generations. This is driving a surge in investment activity, particularly among younger generations, who have been hardest hit and will have the bittersweet experience of financial uncertainty early in life that will move them to invest in their future, rather than spending recklessly.

Prior to the pandemic, I was already working remotely, but now it has become common for more people and it's driving property investment in regional locations. For office workers, it's becoming clear that you don't necessarily have to live in a big city just because your office is there. That means more people have access to decent properties on blocks of land further from the city centres. Those who previously felt locked out of the market in capital cities might be able to move to towns where property is more affordable and set up a flexible working arrangement with their company. I know this is not an option for everyone, but it's opening previously closed doors to home ownership for those who are able to make the shift.

Consumer demand for sustainable managed funds and ETFs

It has never been easier to access sustainable shares with a low initial investment. The apps I've explored allow customers to start investing for less than the cost of a latte and to build on that over time. People who set up automatic direct debits are developing a habit that will become central to their spending philosophy. On the flip side, they're demanding that the contents of these portfolios are ethical, and in future these products will improve both in the quality of the content and in the potential for return as sustainability becomes a non-negotiable aspect of business activity.

Epic wealth transfer

Baby boomers, the wealthiest generation in history, are increasingly handing their funds over to the succeeding generations. Millennials and gen Z are seriously 'woke' when it comes to social and environmental issues. Expect those who are lucky enough to receive a considerable inheritance to not only move the needle in the ethical investments they make, but push it to the end of the spectrum for maximum benefit.

Let's get ethical

In late 2021, I got on Instagram and searched the hashtag 'ethical investing'. There is so much information on social media about the topic. Obviously, you need to make your own decisions, but it's something people around the world are talking about. Back when I was in my twenties, people were mostly posting selfies and photos of their food. Naturally, they're still doing that, but now there's a generation of young investors talking transparently about their strategies. There's a hell of a lot of self-taught people who are sharing what they've learned.

I certainly don't treat this type of content as financial advice, but I do treat it as inspiration. My worldview has expanded, and I find out about opportunities that might be right for my ethical approach. I can't tell you how you should invest, but I can share some personal advice from my experience: don't be too hard on yourself if you're striving to build an ethical and sustainable financial life. It is exceedingly difficult to be 'perfect'. Getting started and simply viewing your finances from an ethical standpoint is an excellent first step. At several moments in this process, I've beaten myself up for not having green-enough investments. Now I realise that I'm doing more than the average punter simply by trying. Making small sustainable changes in your own backyard is better than doing nothing at all. I'll tell anyone who'll listen to go and look at the contents of their superannuation. I'll happily explain the benefits of ethical investment to those who are interested. I hope that, at a minimum, the message continues to spread.

This is only the beginning of a significant economic shift. Remember the early years of the internet, when a website full of fluorescent Comic Sans font was the height of sophistication? That's kind of where we are now. We're just learning how to use ethical investment for the most impact, learning to design more innovative tools to support it, building businesses that will later become outstanding investments. I hope, in twenty years from now, we'll look back at the early 2020s and ethical investment will be as omnipresent as the internet is now. I wonder if those of us who start now will look back and say, 'Wow, I can't believe so few people were doing it. It was so obvious.'

For now, I'll continue to research, invest where I can and simply be pleased that I've started. And when I'm not investing, I'll be in my garden, tending to my tomatoes. Growing your wealth is just like planting fruit and veg. First, you've got what feels like nothing but a couple of seeds and a pile of dirt, then, over time, you have a flourishing and nourishing portfolio. I wish you the best of luck on your ethical investing path. I hope you find it as rewarding as I have.

Acknowledgements

Most people don't write books while they're learning about the subject along the way, but my publisher, Sophy Williams, thought I could do it. Thanks Sophy for taking a punt on me, and the world of ethical investment. I feel so fortunate to have had this opportunity and I'm grateful to be able to pass my knowledge on. I really hope it makes a difference.

To the team at Black Inc., you guys rock. Thanks in particular to my editor, Kate Morgan. Your wonderful eye and easy nature have made this process a dream. Caraline Douglas and Pam Rupasinghe, you know how much I love Instagram, thanks for your digital marketing prowess. Sallie Butler, I'm stoked to have been able to work with you to share this message, too. Alex Adsett, how lucky I am to have an agent who I can call a friend. Thank you as always for your enthusiasm and chats about our cats.

Writing a book is hard. Writing a book during a pandemic while selling a property, buying a new one, moving and starting a renovation is lunacy-level behaviour. I was only able to do this thanks to an extraordinary support network, in particular Kate Vines who helped me during my Ballarat purchase process, and Margot Bourchier who took me straight to Bunnings on arrival. Also, those who propped me up when I didn't think I could keep going: my parents Sharyn and Colin, brothers Paul and Joel, my (practically) sister-in-law Christine Stone, and friends Beck Thiso and Sally Wright.

Moving to a regional town alone took a massive leap of faith. To those who made Ballarat feel like home almost instantly: Katherine White and Brooke Lyons, I'm indebted. Thanks Kat, for the constant reno chats and the local immersion, and Brooke for offering to read my early pages – you're a magnificent editor.

A book like this doesn't come together without remarkable people giving their time and being incredibly vulnerable, sharing personal financial information. Thank you to every single interviewee who chatted to me. There are too many of you to thank here, but please know that it's appreciated and I hope it helps other aspiring ethical investors move forward.

Finally, Peach and Olive, you'll never read this because you're cats, but I want it on paper that having you snooze next to me while I write makes all the difference.

Index